Empowering Words

Adult Coloring Book
for Stress Relief & Relaxation

Thomas Calabris

Empowering Words
Publisher: Inner Vitality Systems, LLC
Website: www.InnerVitalitySystems.com

Let The Relaxation Begin

Inside you will find **50 beautiful empowering word designs**. You will also find inspiring quotes on the alternate pages. Let go and be in the present moment as you bring the artwork to life with color. It is as much about the journey as the destination. **Relax** into the present moment as you color, allowing the stress and tension to melt away. Take a deep breath and enjoy!

I recommend using colored pencils because they will give you the best precision to color the small intricate details when sharpened. Crayons may also be used, but I recommend that you sharpen them. If you choose to use colored markers, gel pens, or other wet medium, please place a piece of cardboard behind the image you are coloring to prevent them from bleeding through to the next page.

Visit **InnerVitalitySystems.com/AdultColoringBookForStressRelief** to download another printable coloring book (in pdf format) for free. Also, please leave a comment and a review if you enjoy this coloring book.

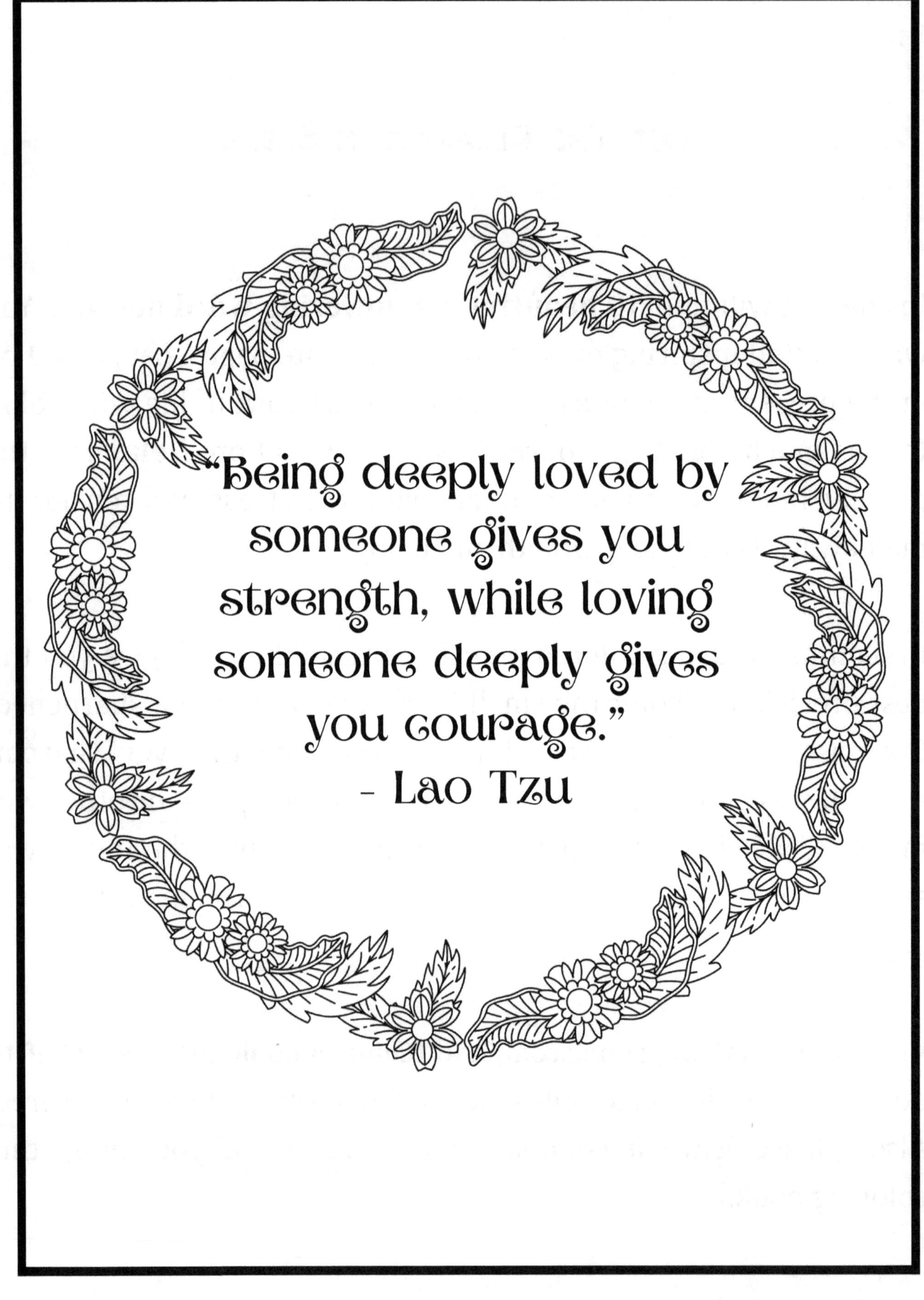
"Being deeply loved by
someone gives you
strength, while loving
someone deeply gives
you courage."
- Lao Tzu

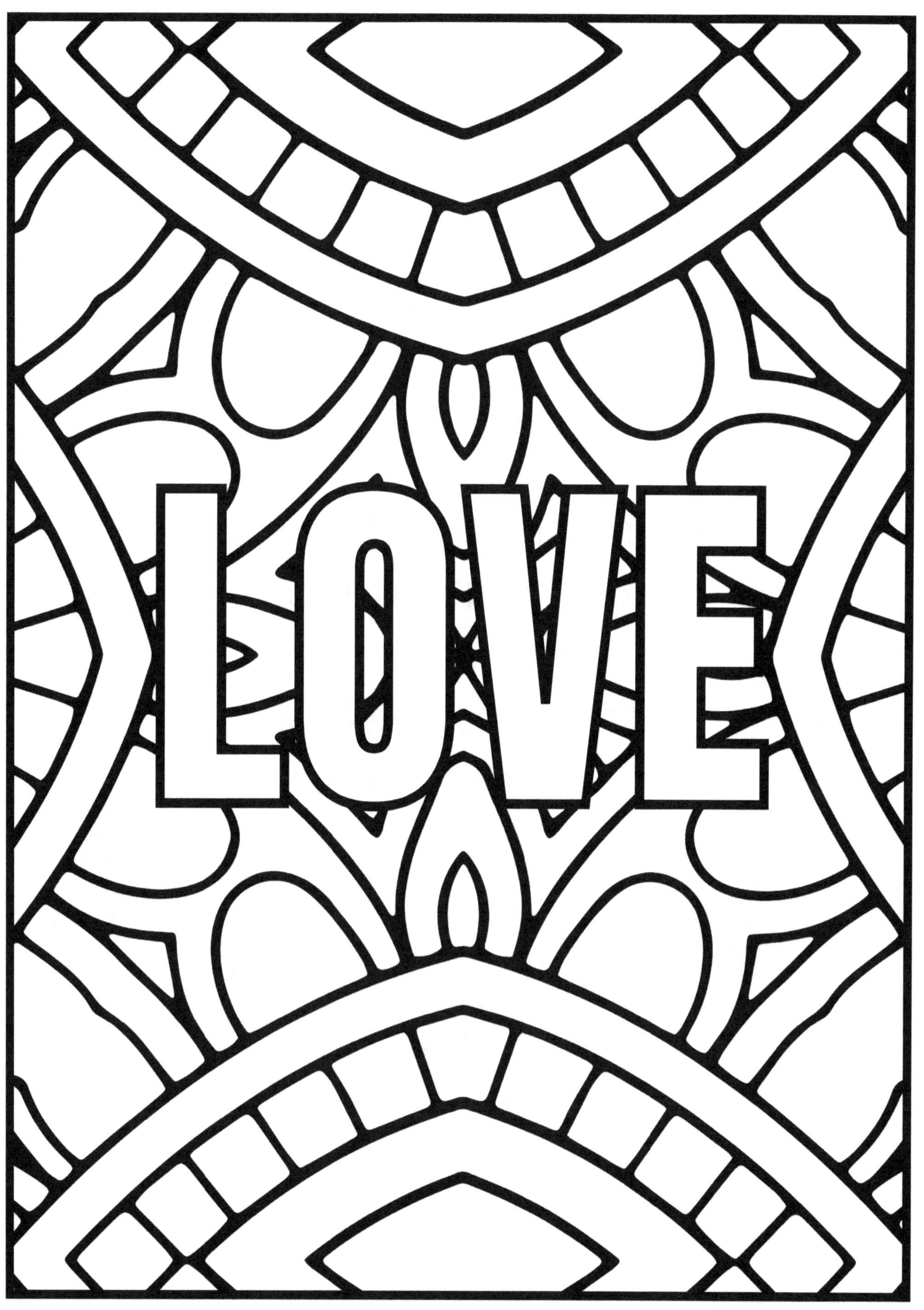
LOVE

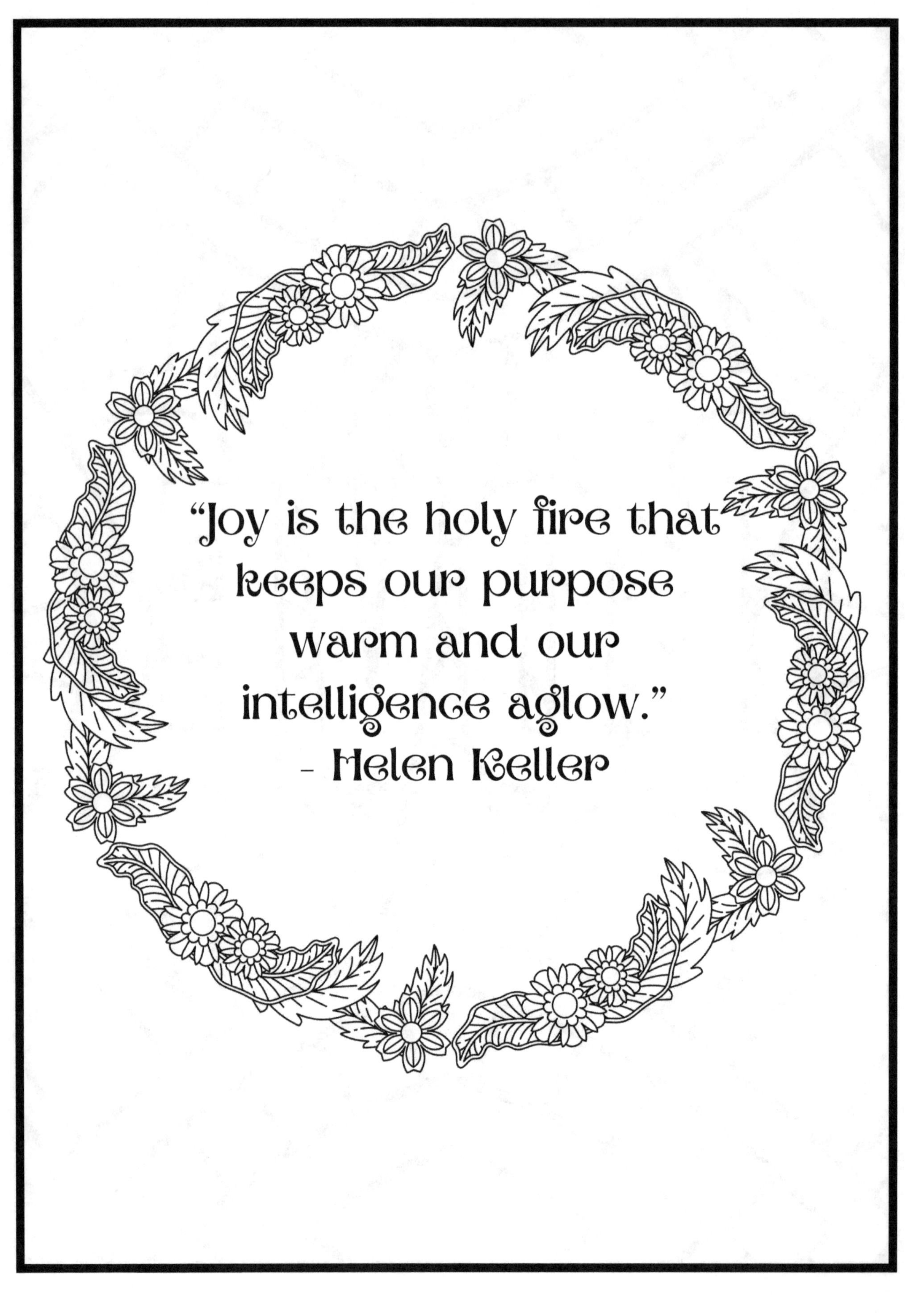
"Joy is the holy fire that
keeps our purpose
warm and our
intelligence aglow."
- Helen Keller

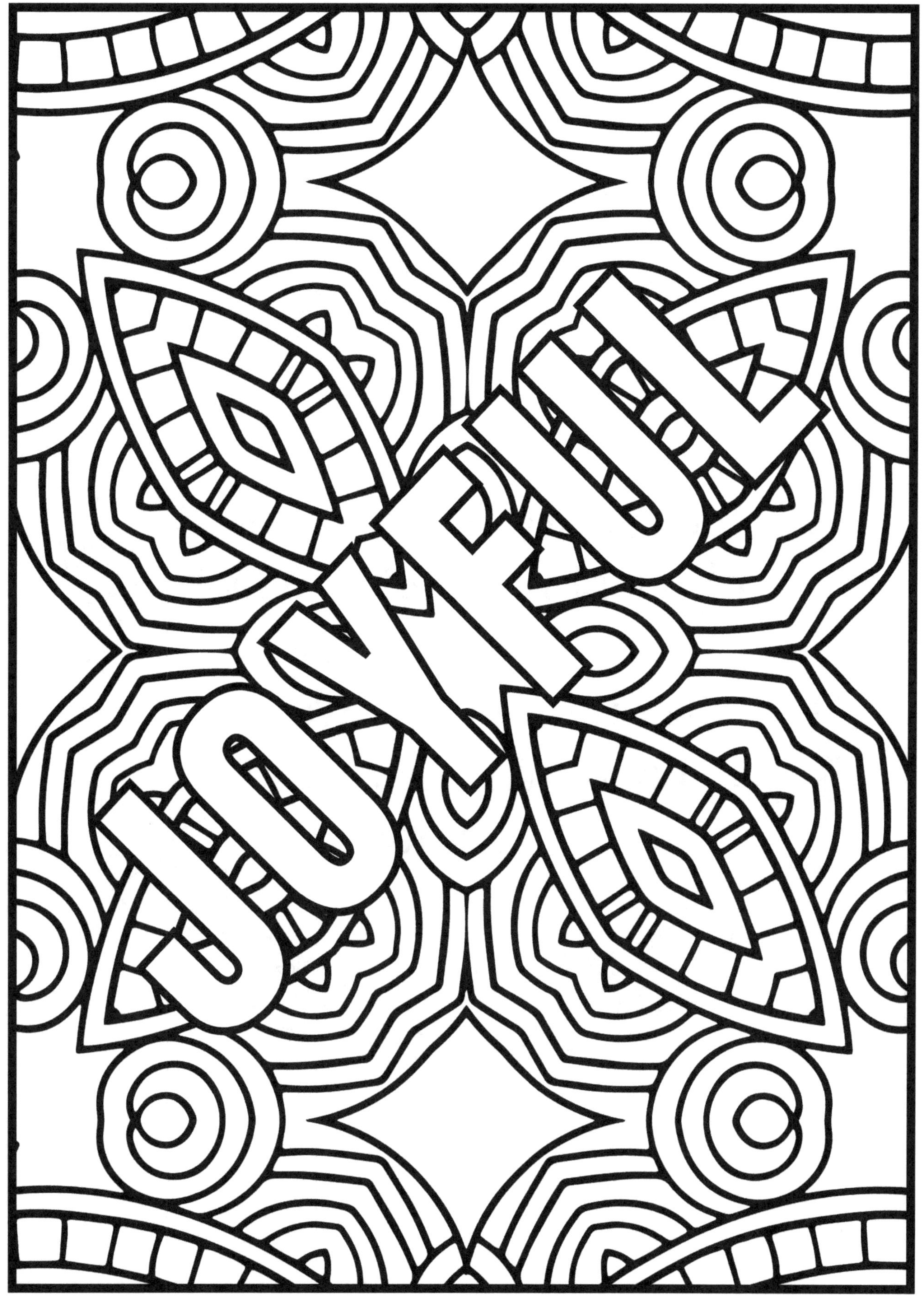
JOYFUL

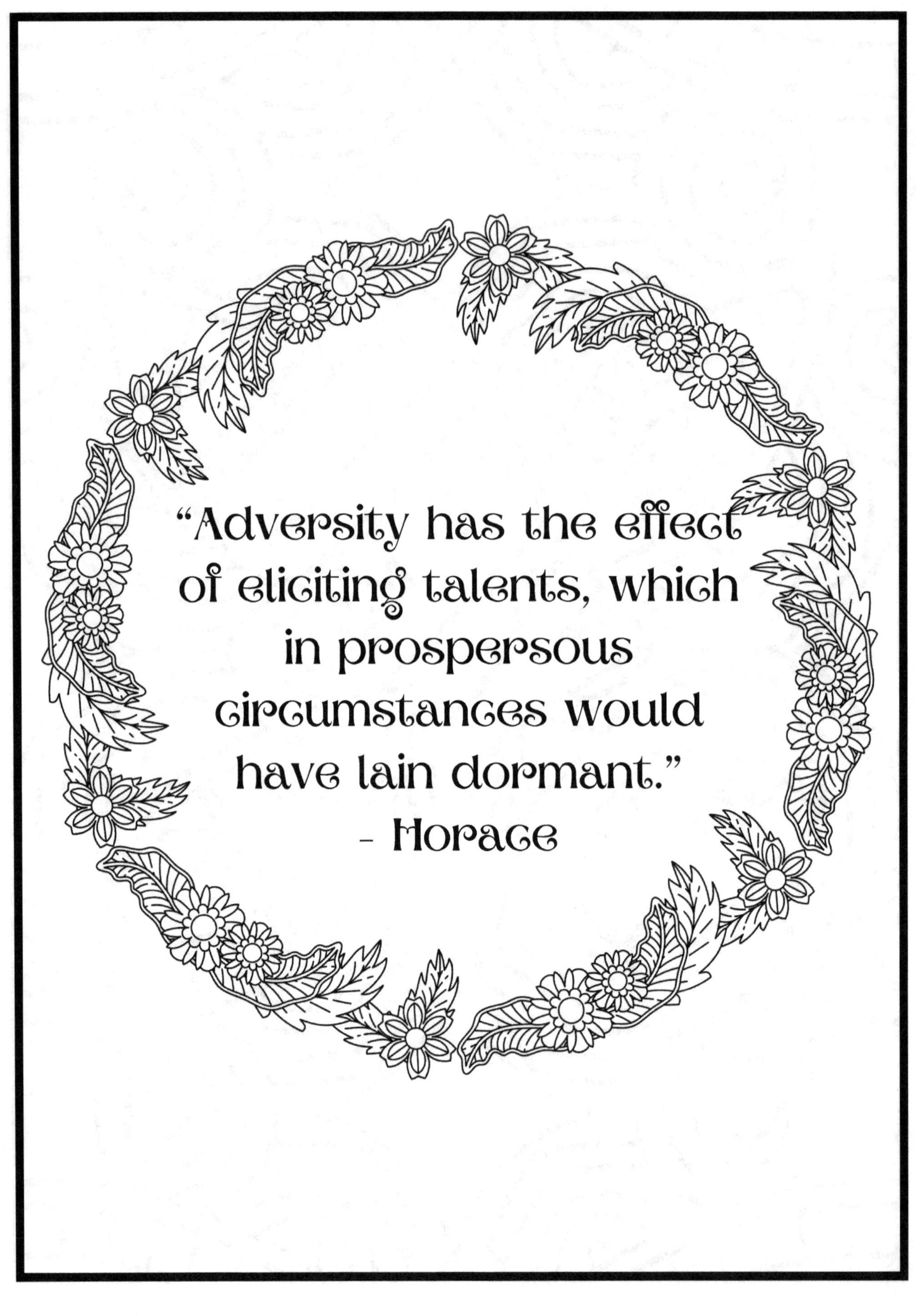
"Adversity has the effect
of eliciting talents, which
in prospersous
circumstances would
have lain dormant."
- Horace

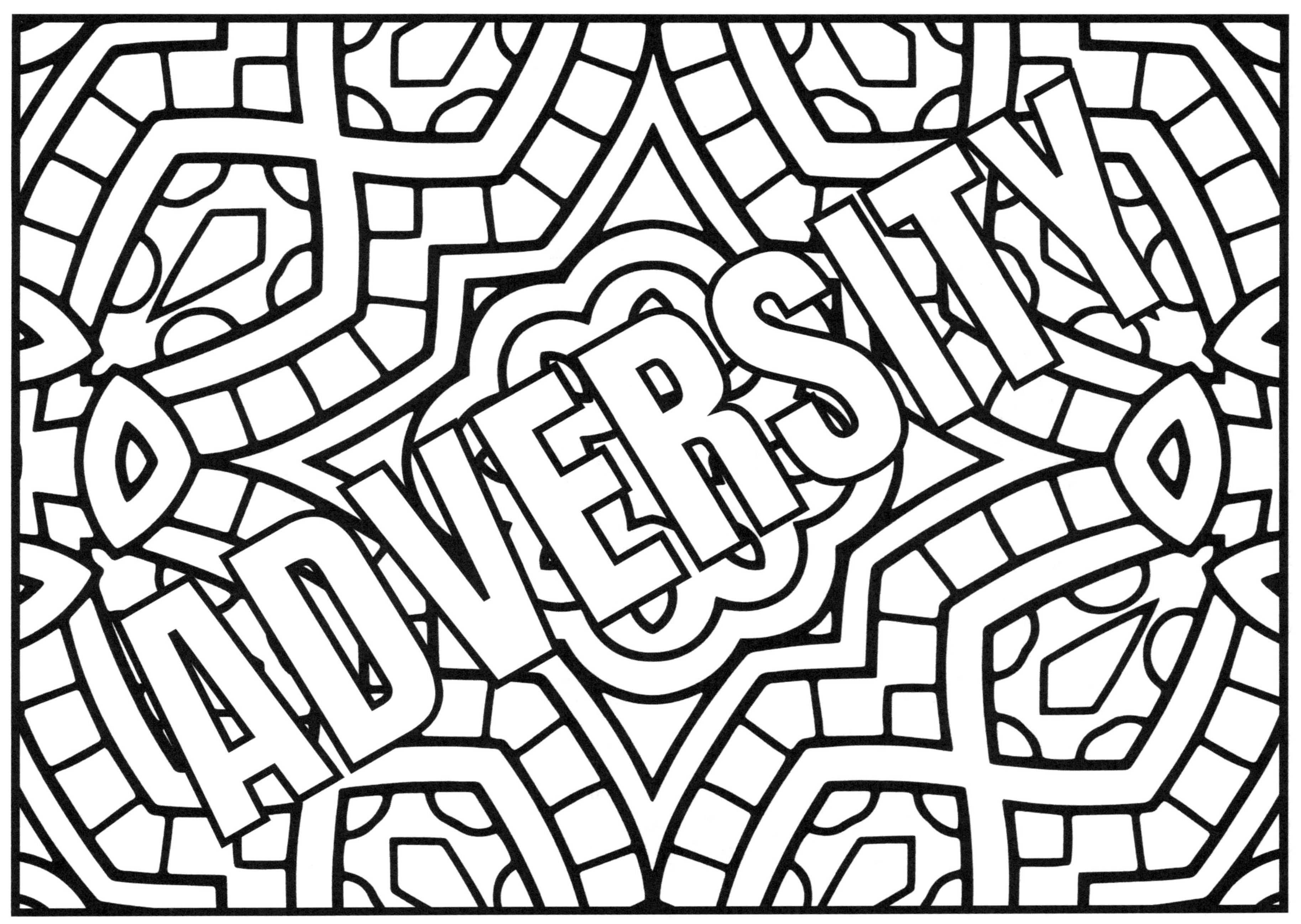
ADVERSITY

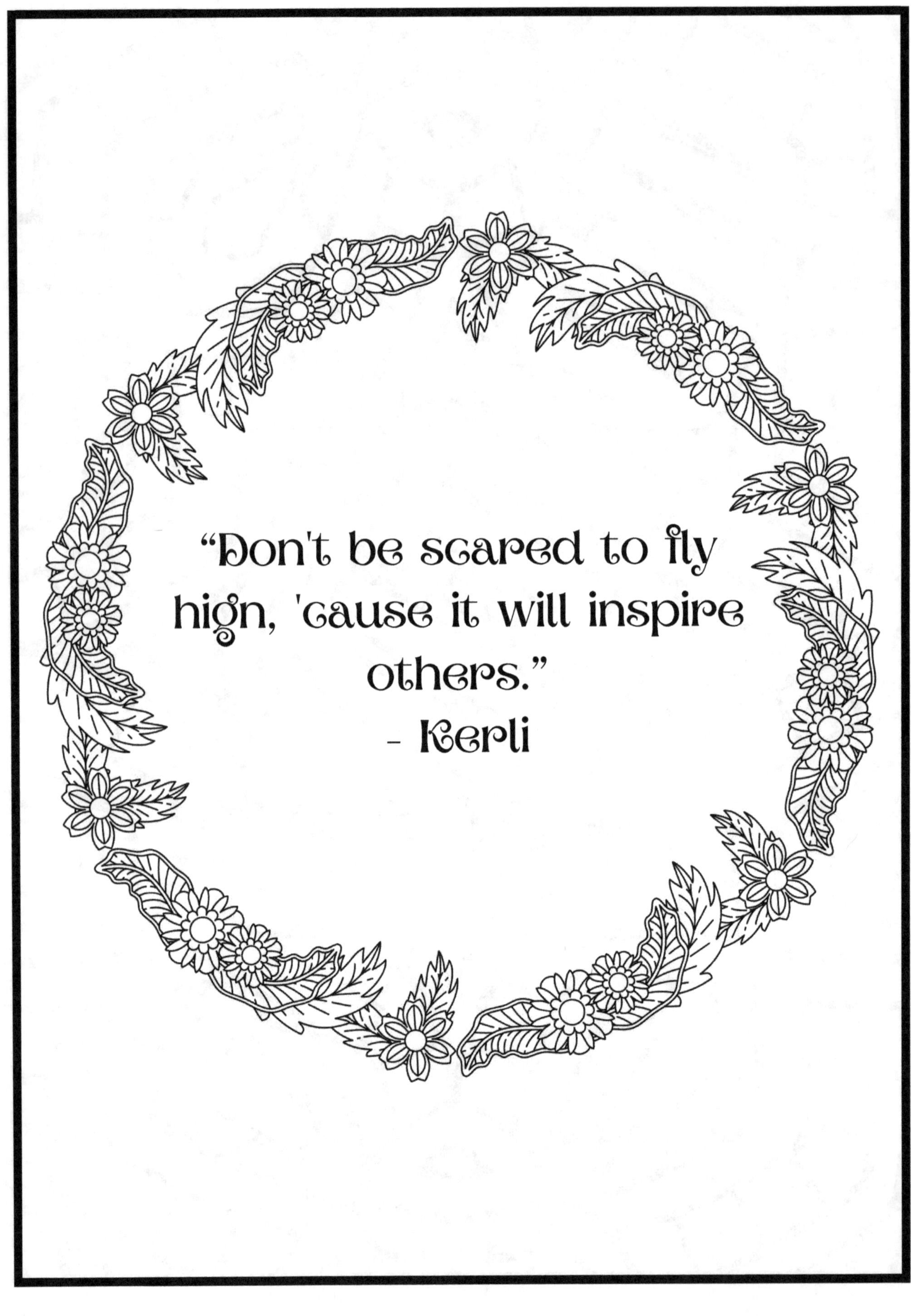
"Don't be scared to fly hign, 'cause it will inspire others."
- Kerli

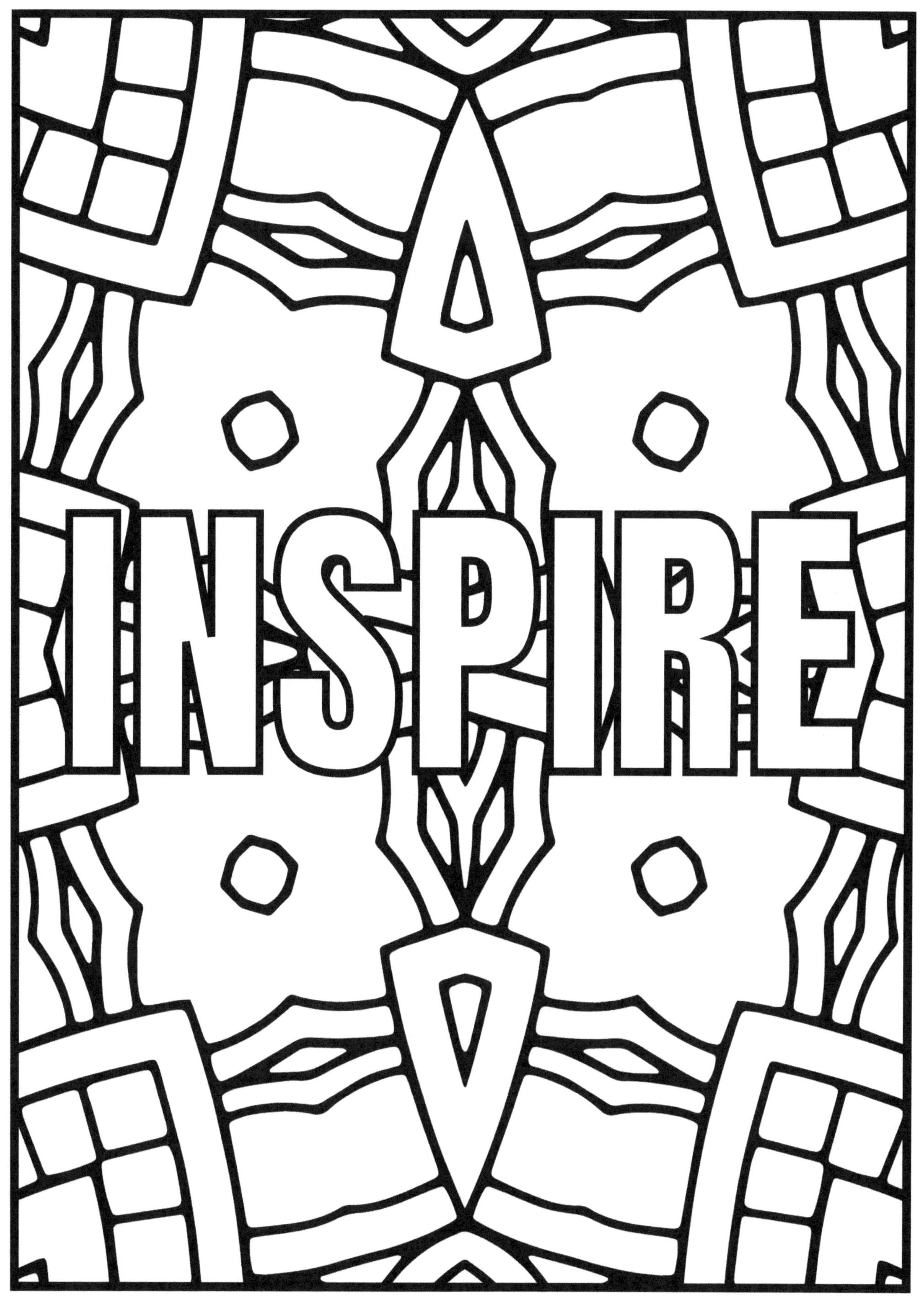
INSPIRE

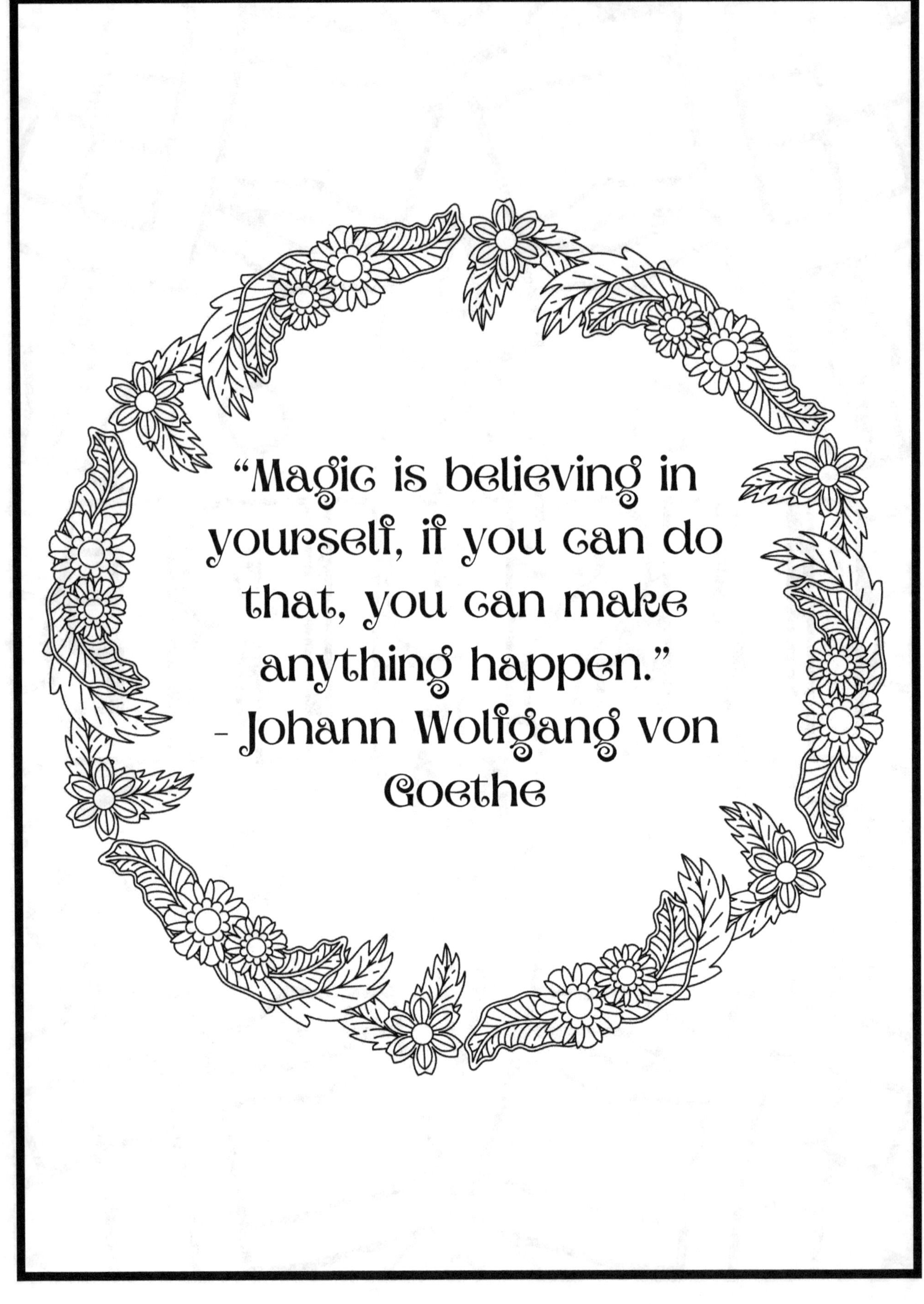
"Magic is believing in
yourself, if you can do
that, you can make
anything happen."
- Johann Wolfgang von
Goethe

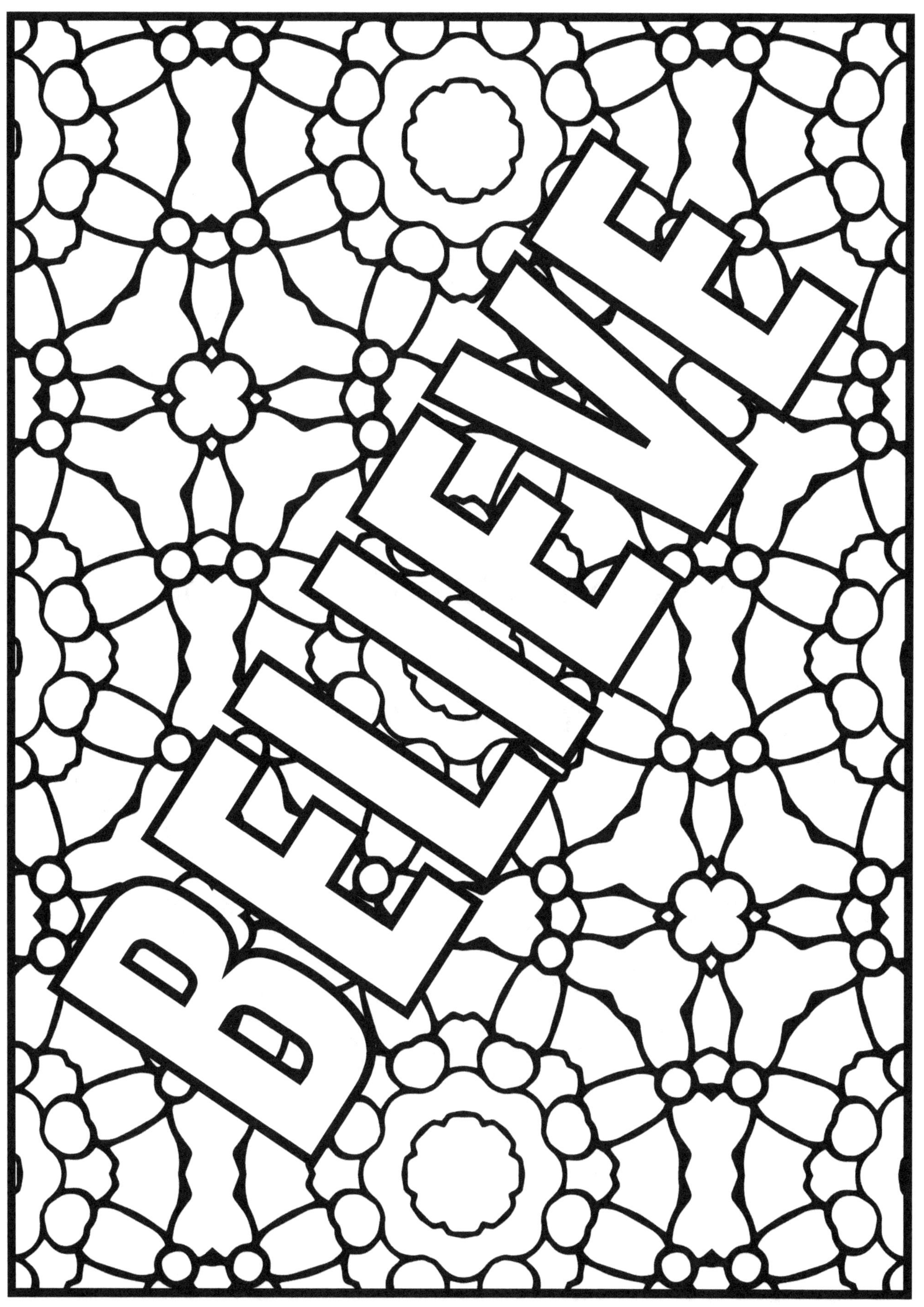
BELIEVE

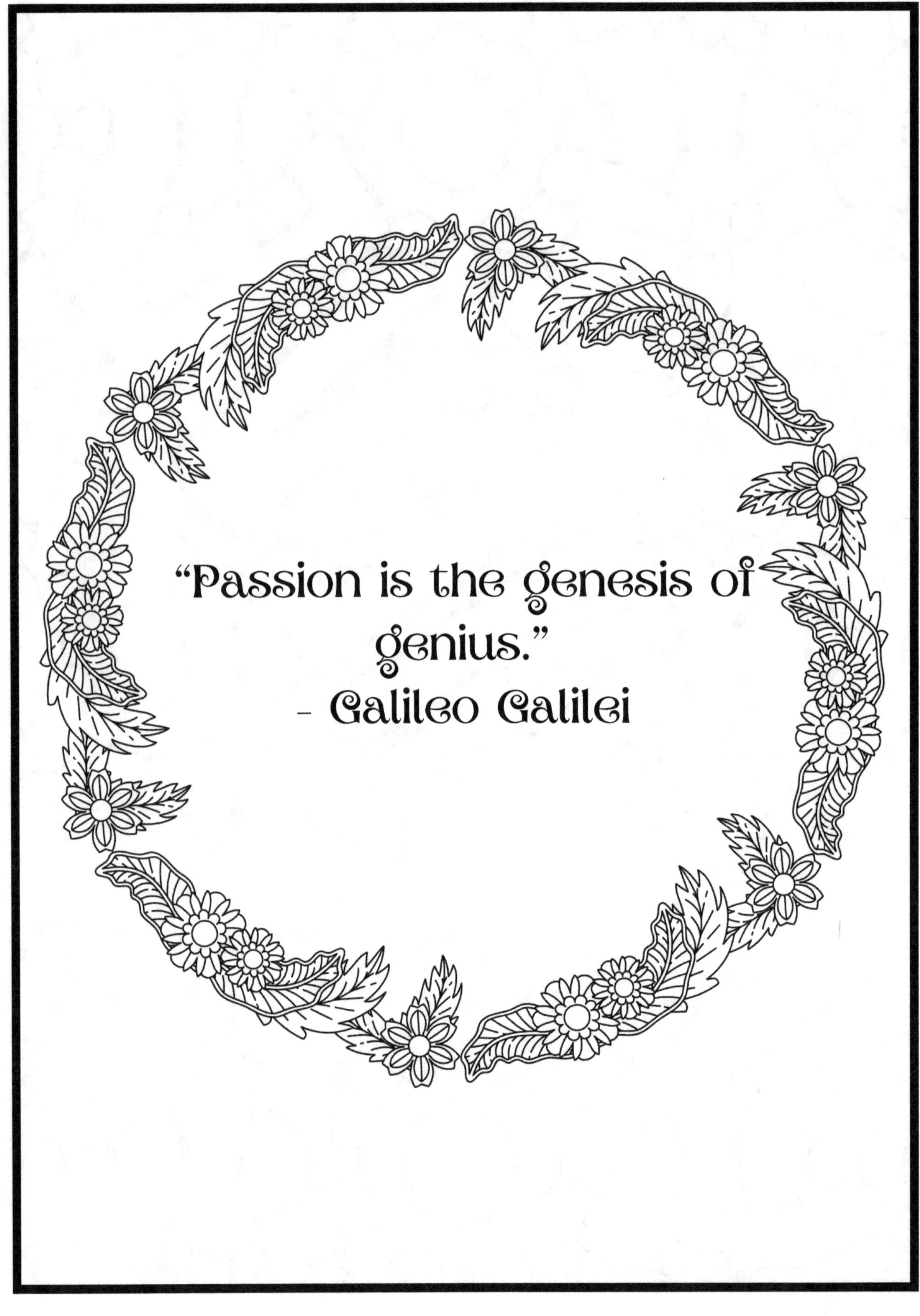
"Passion is the genesis of genius."
- Galileo Galilei

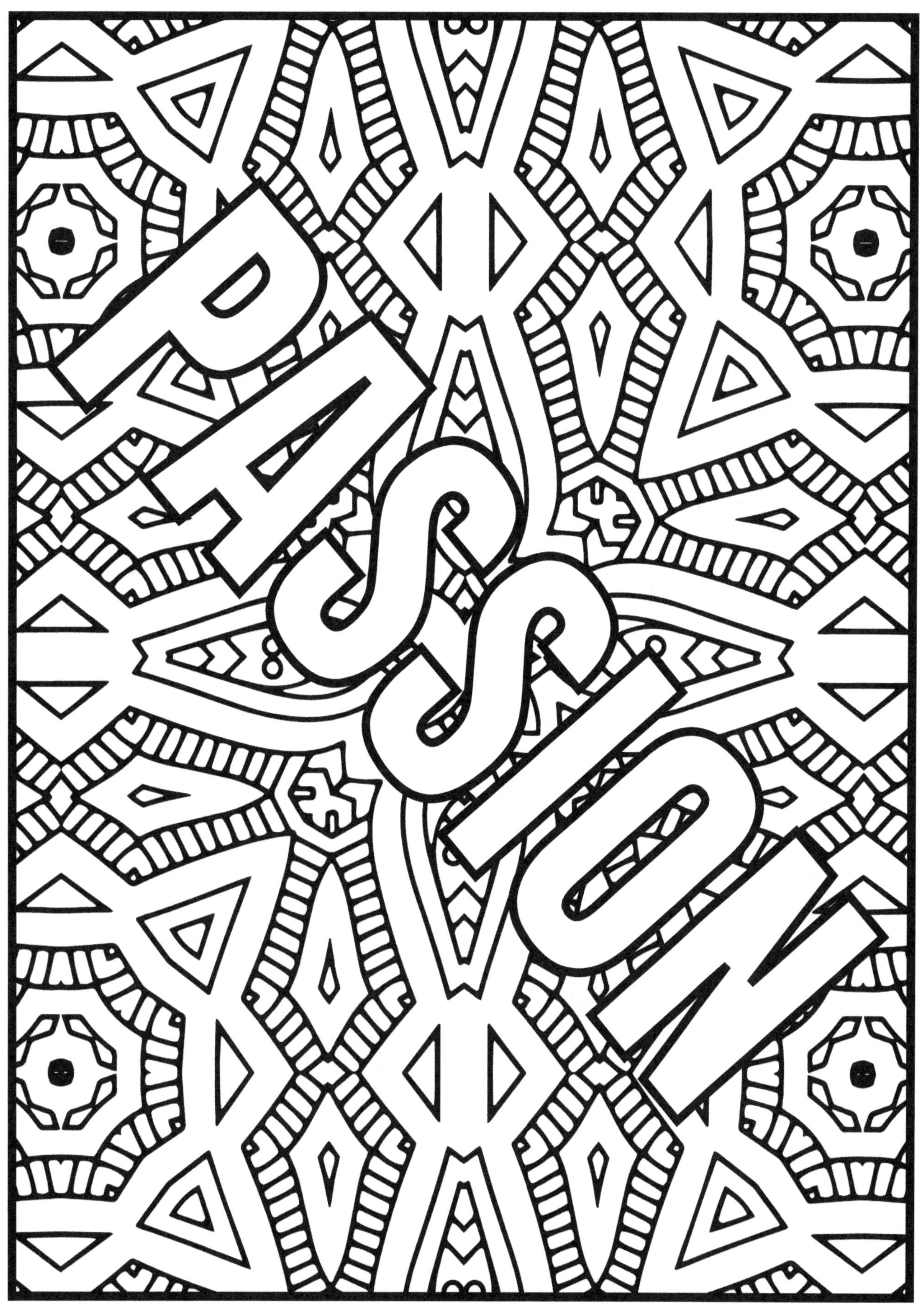
PASSION

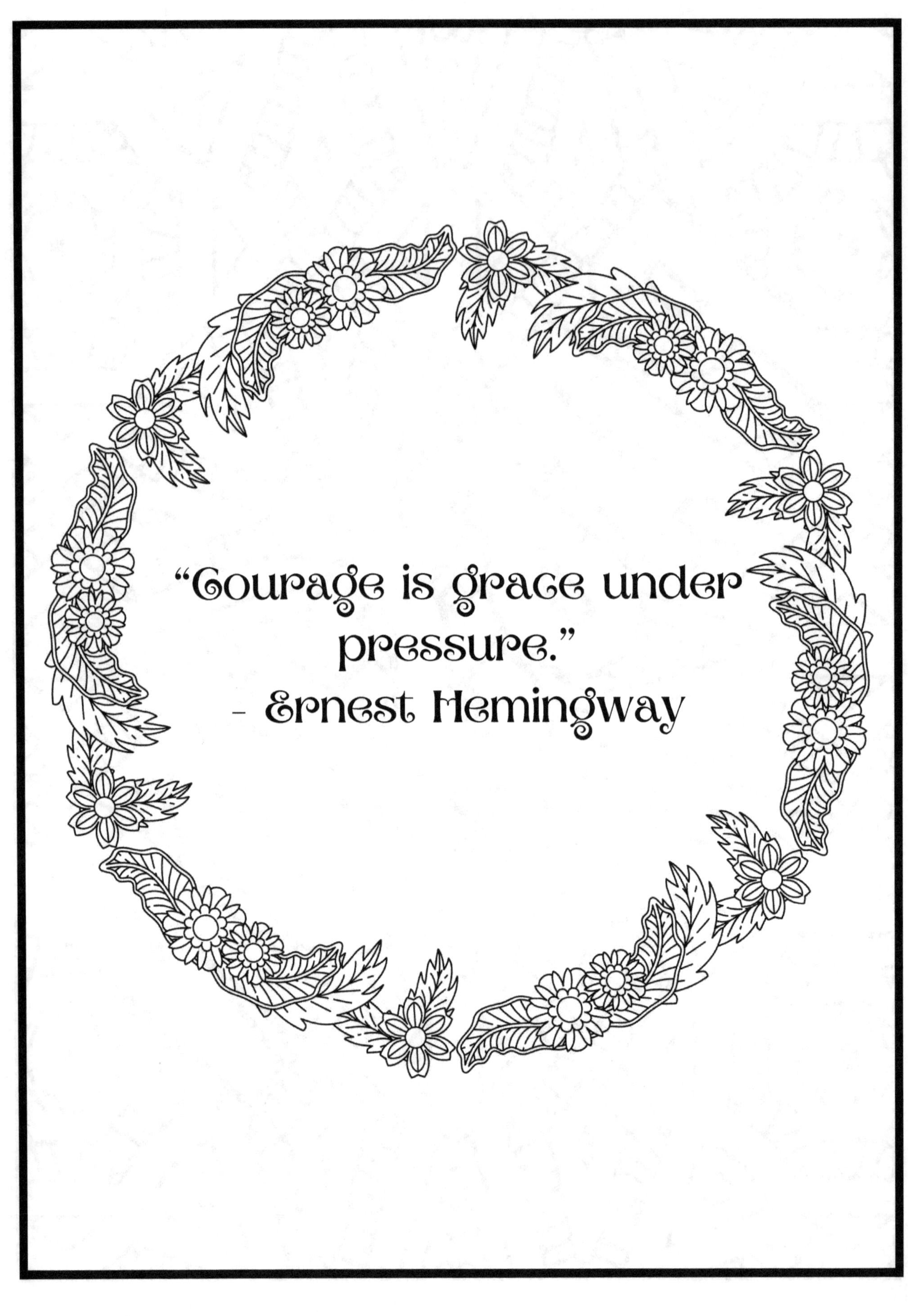
"Courage is grace under pressure."
- Ernest Hemingway

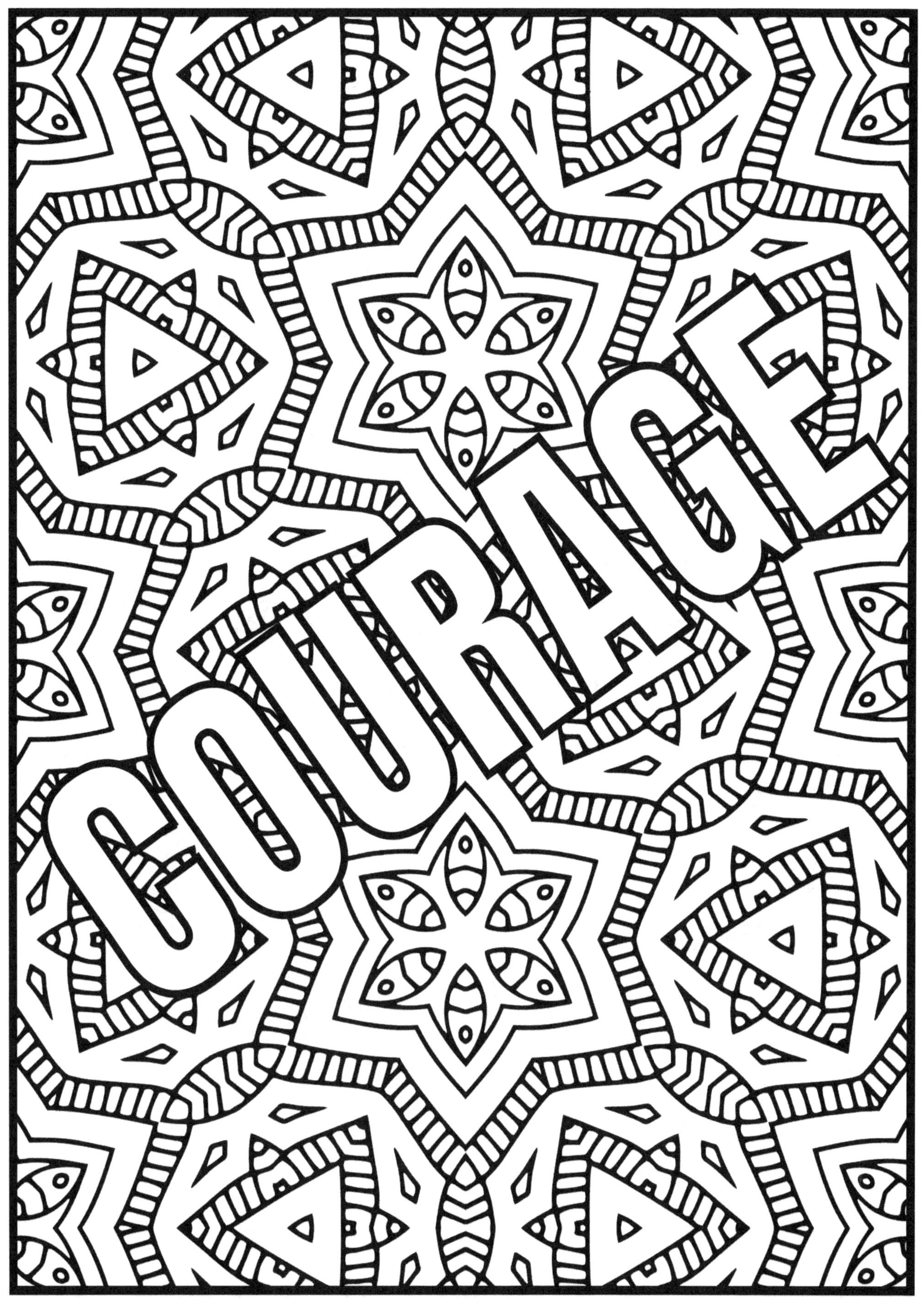
COURAGE

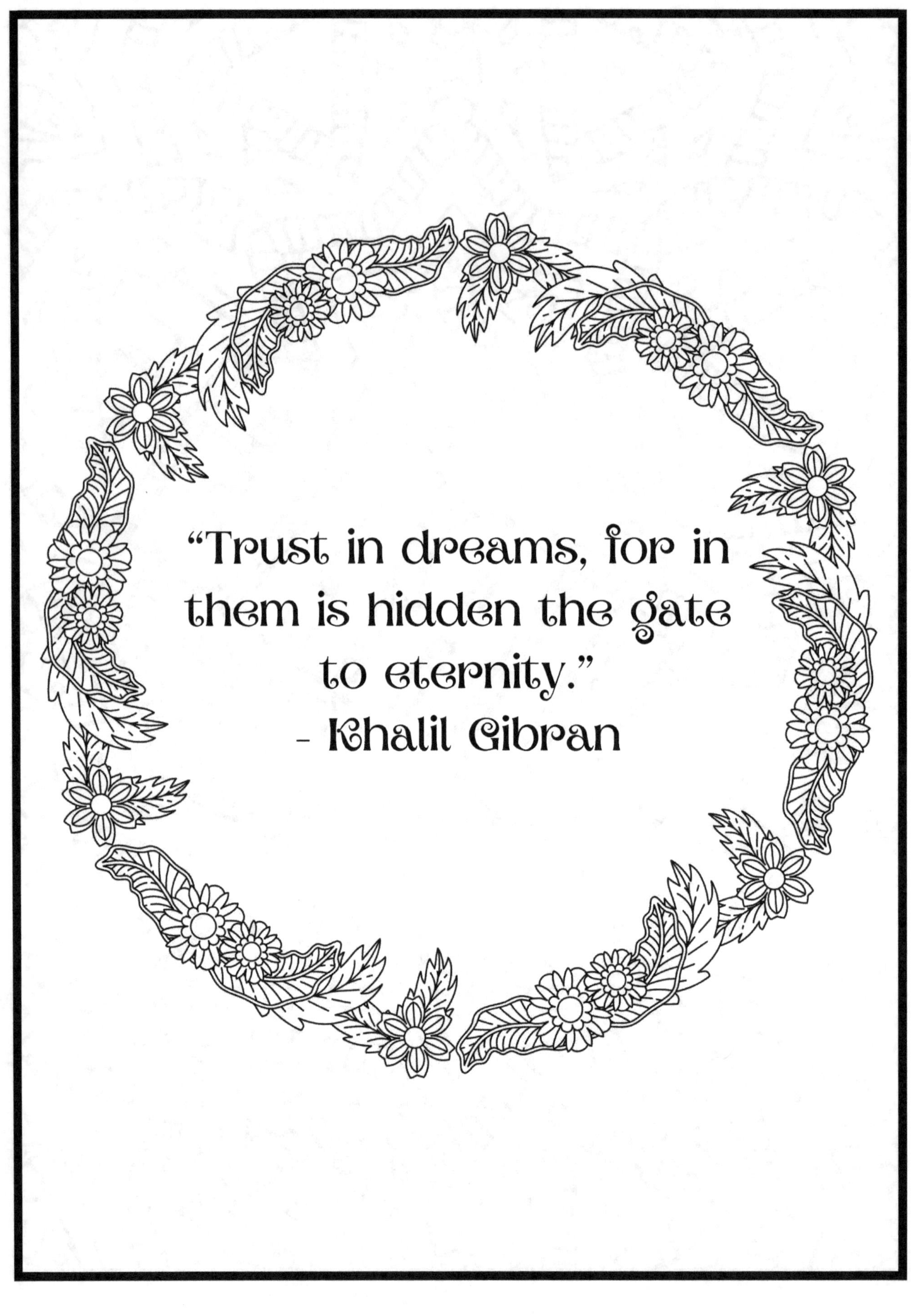
"Trust in dreams, for in
them is hidden the gate
to eternity."
- Khalil Gibran

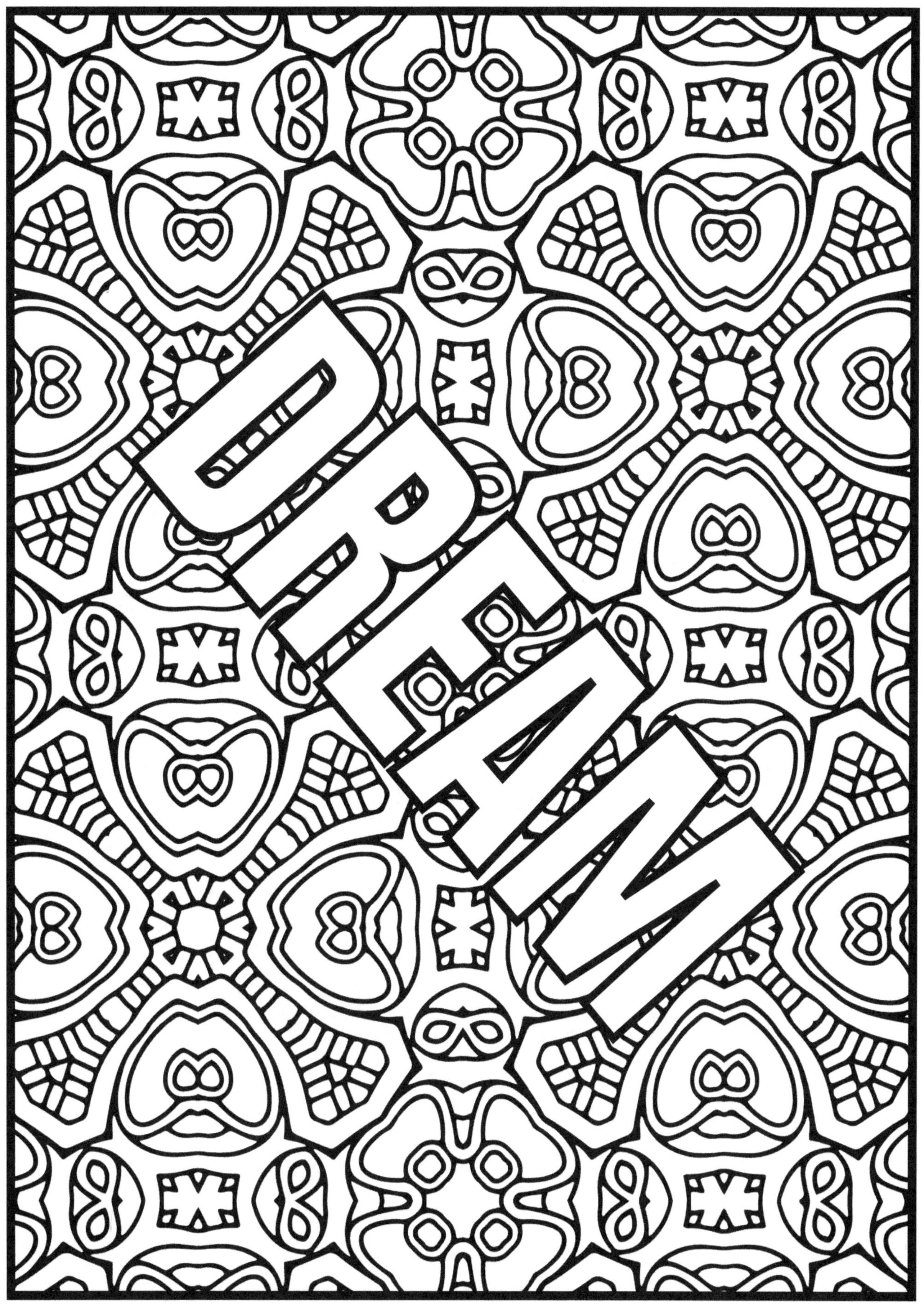
DREAM

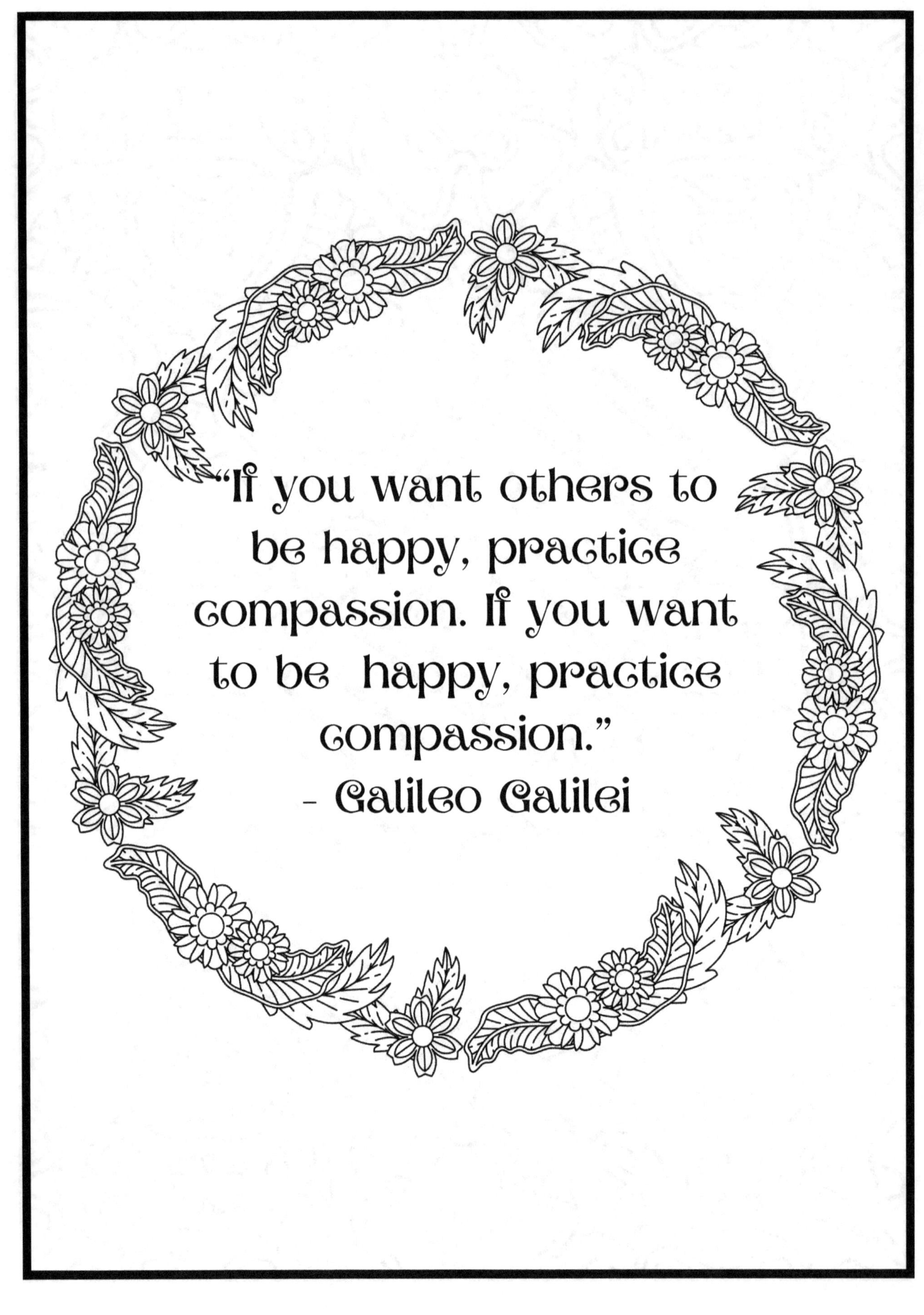
"If you want others to
be happy, practice
compassion. If you want
to be happy, practice
compassion."
- Galileo Galilei

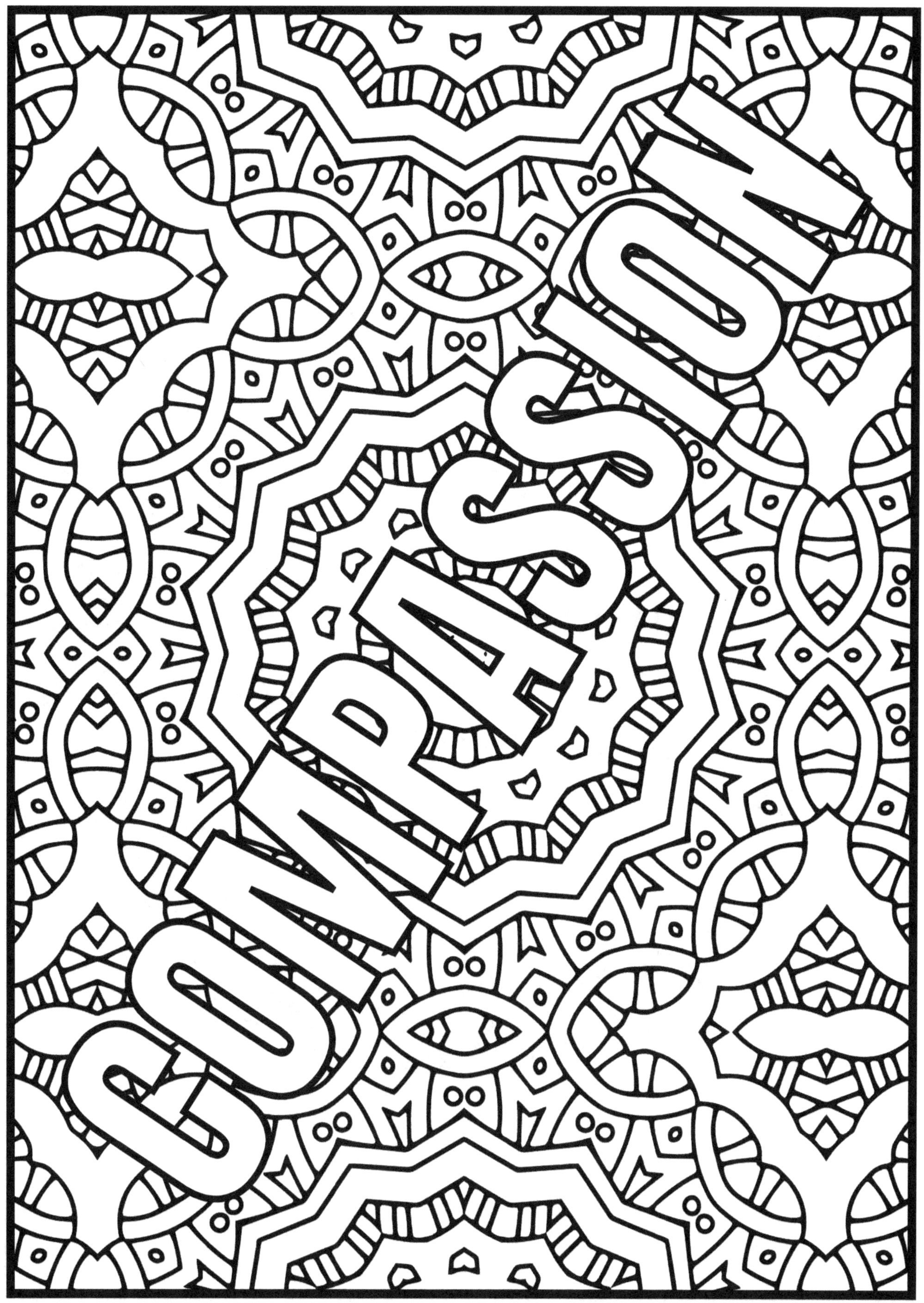
COMPASSION

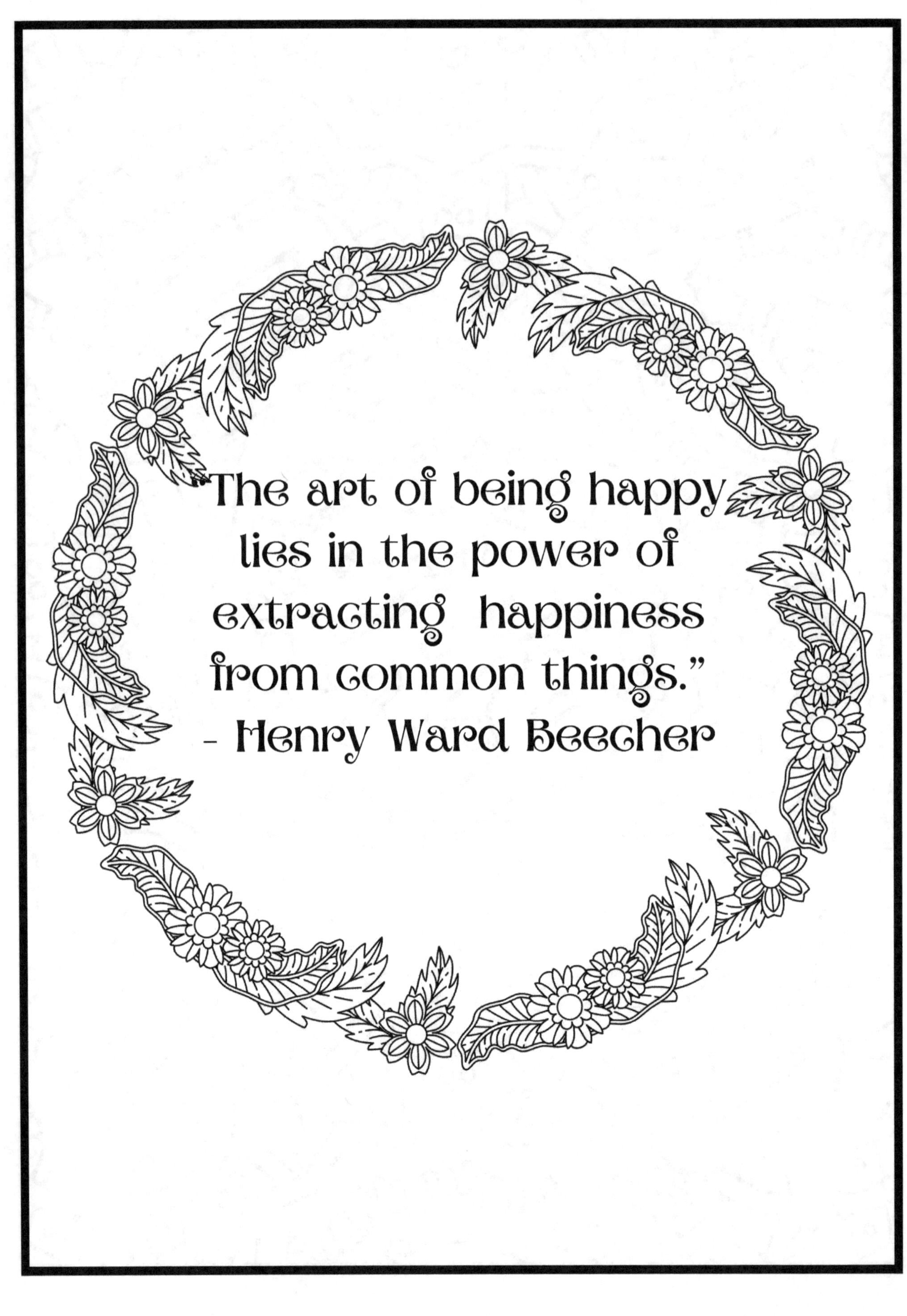
"The art of being happy
lies in the power of
extracting happiness
from common things."
- Henry Ward Beecher

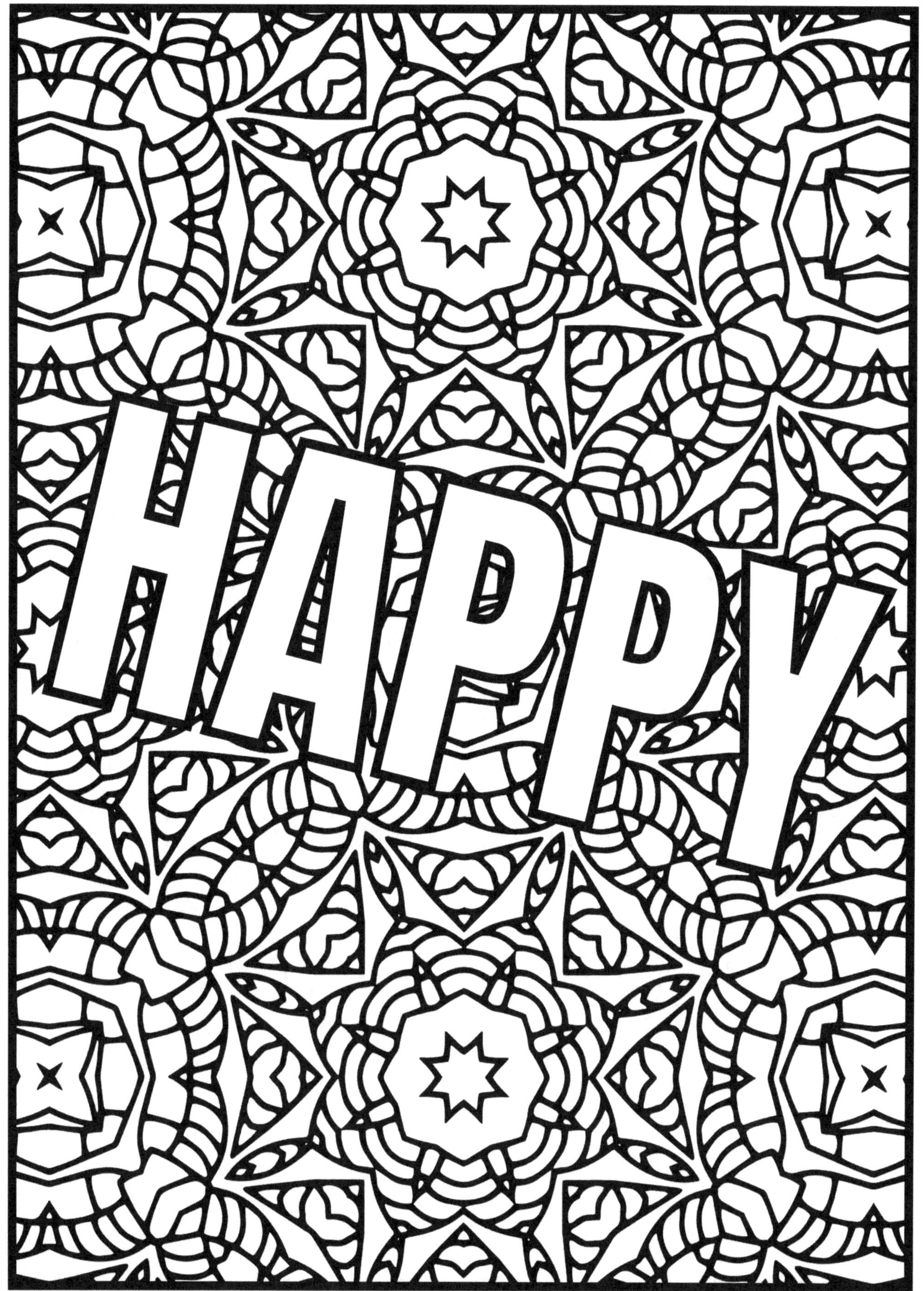
HAPPY

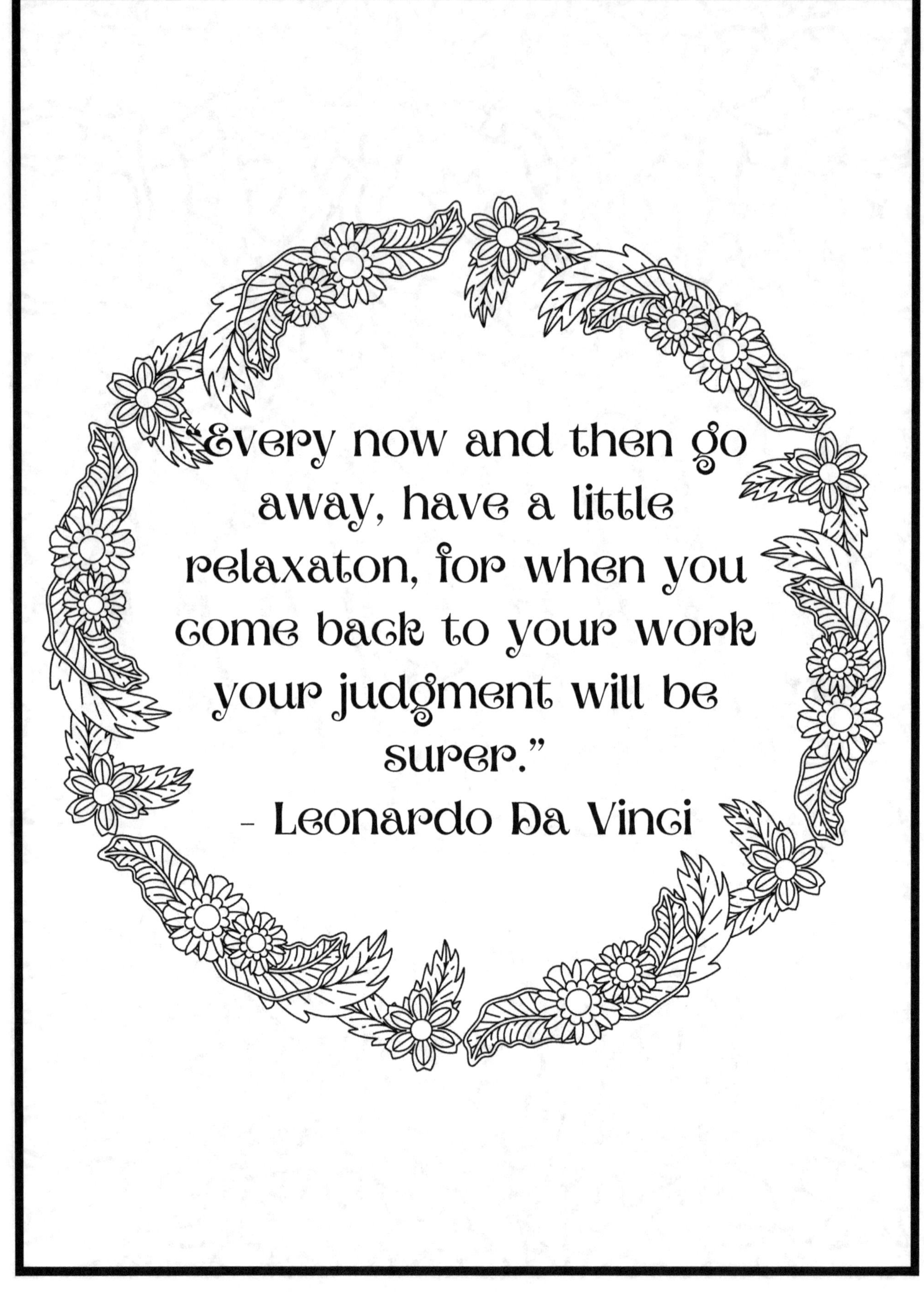
"Every now and then go away, have a little relaxaton, for when you come back to your work your judgment will be surer."
- Leonardo Da Vinci

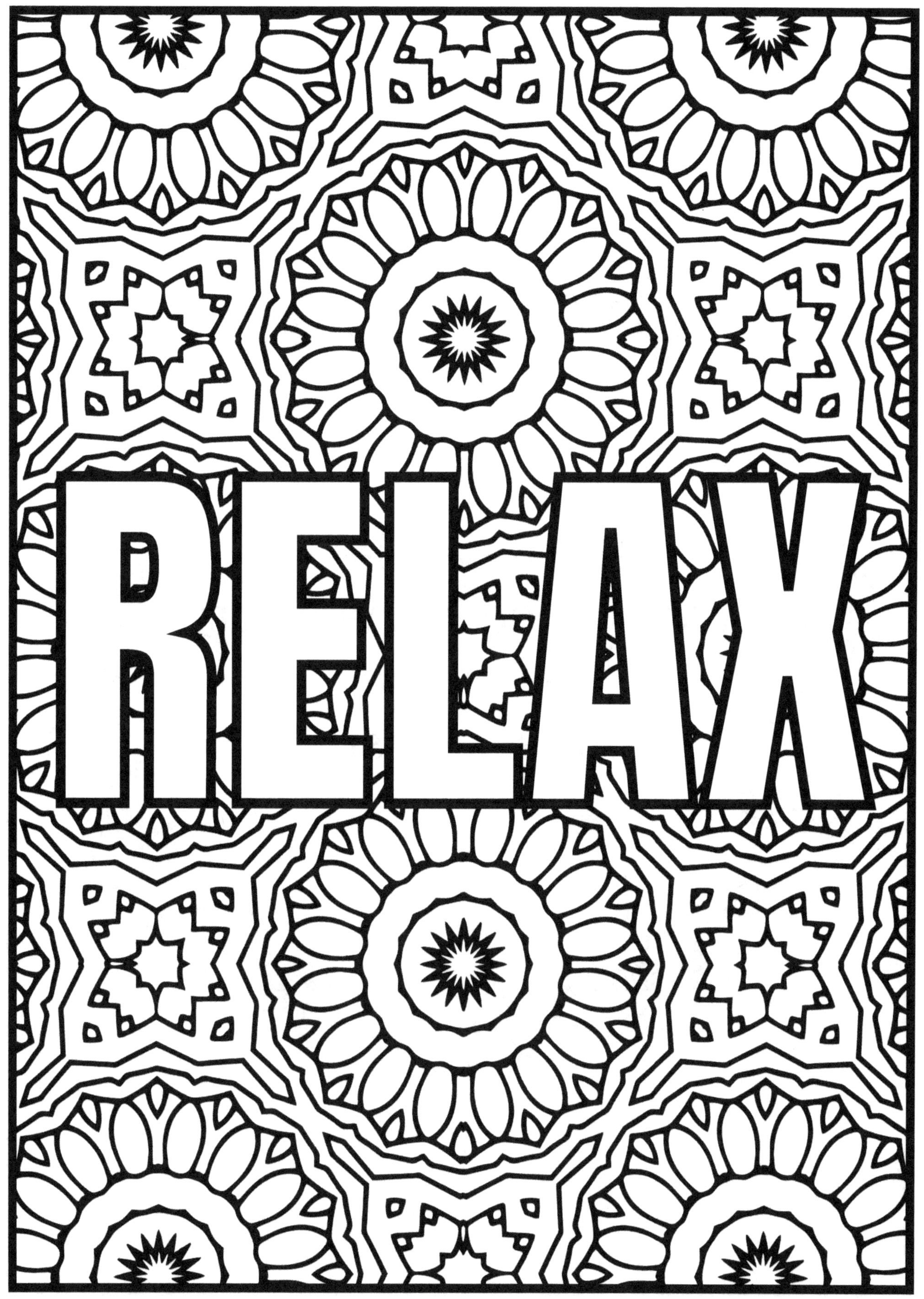
RELAX

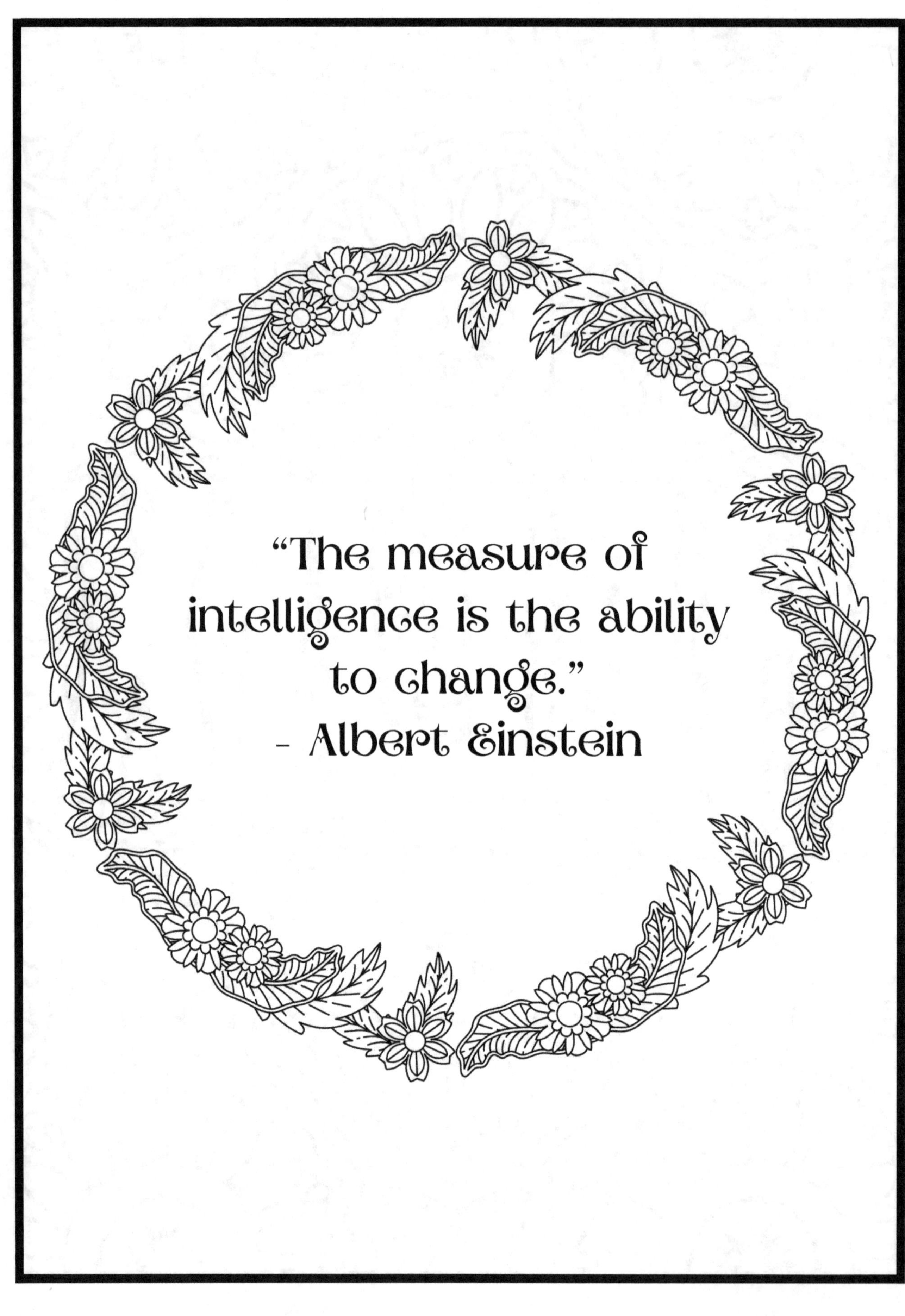
"The measure of
intelligence is the ability
to change."
- Albert Einstein

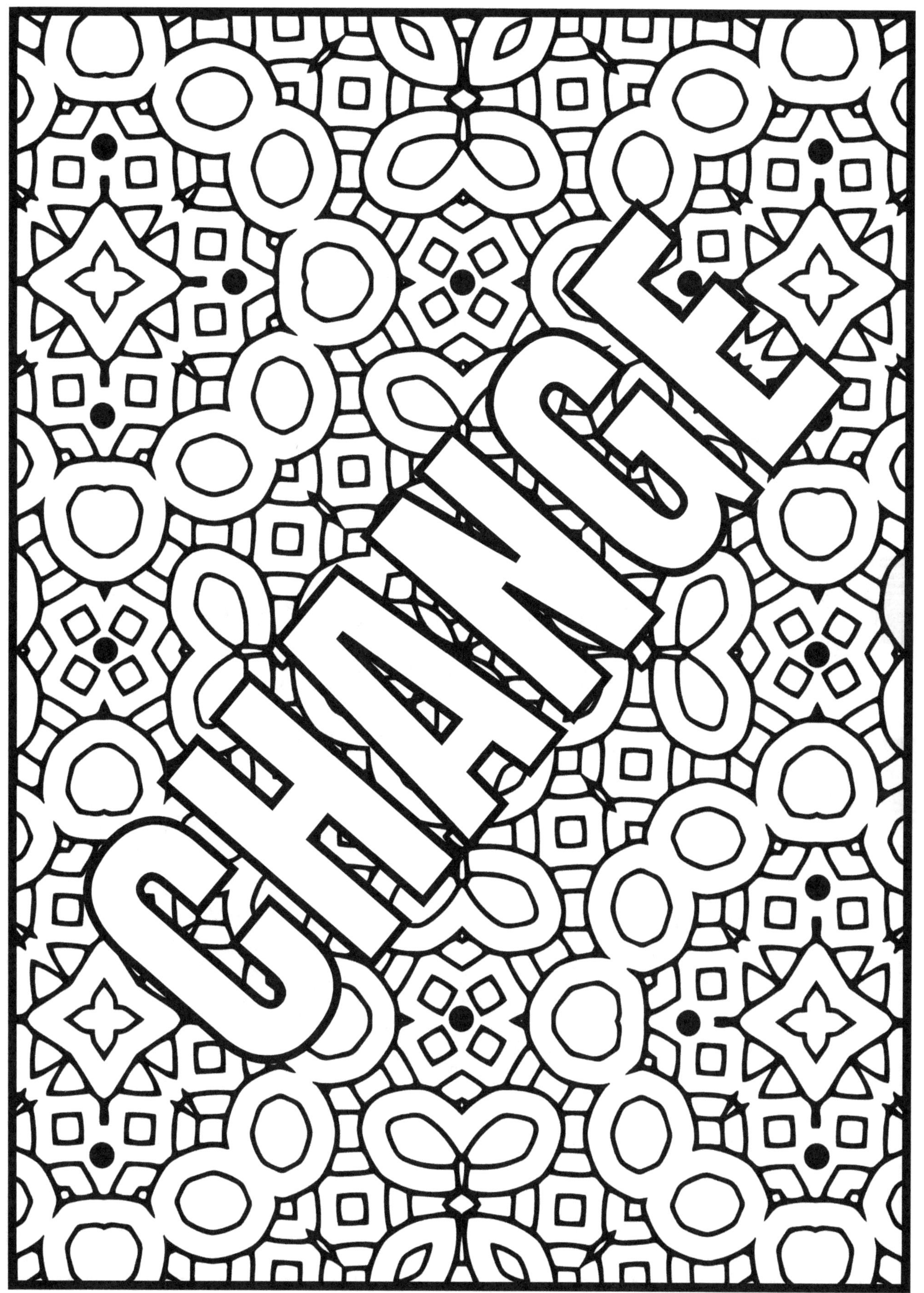
CHANGE

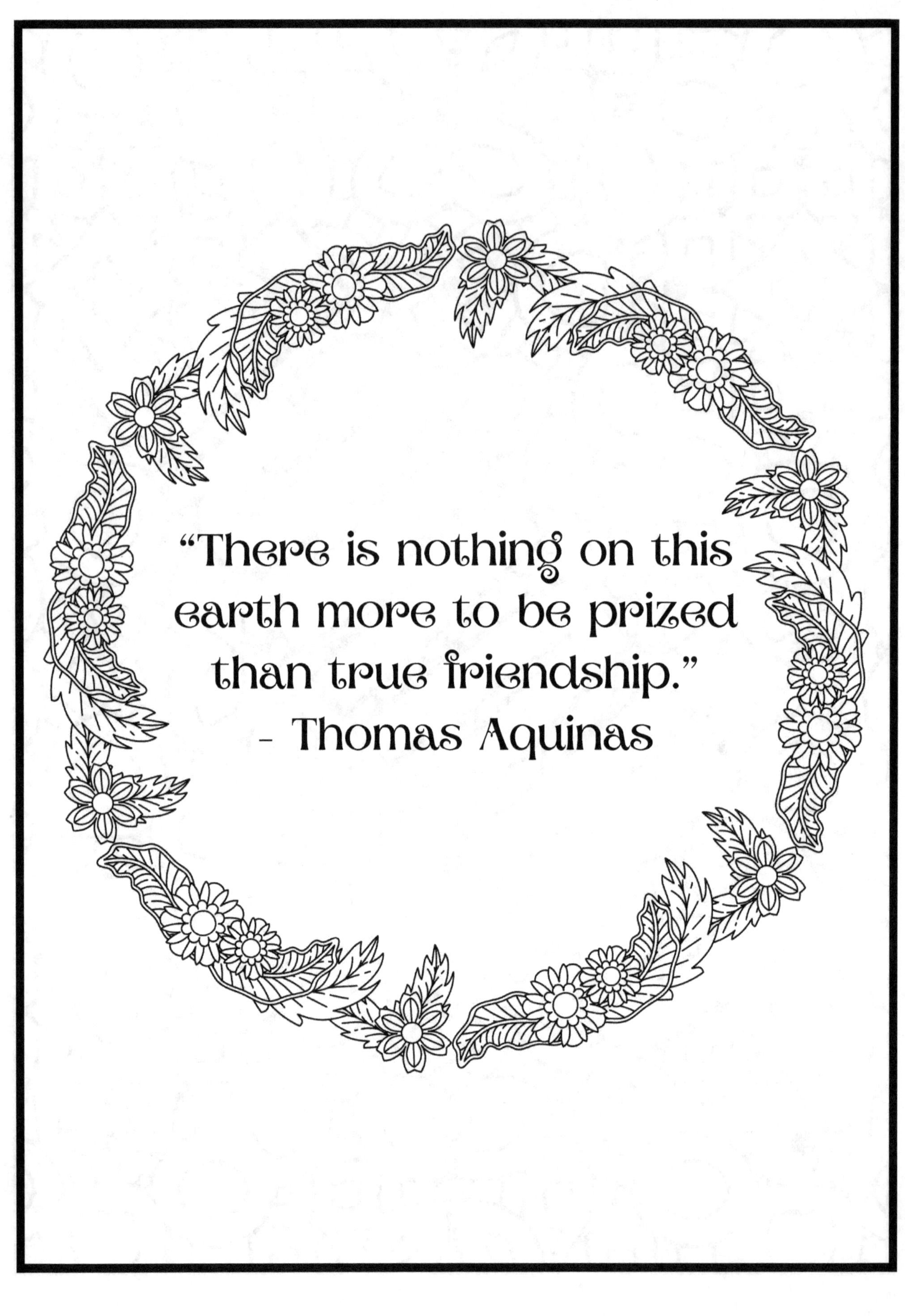
"There is nothing on this
earth more to be prized
than true friendship."
- Thomas Aquinas

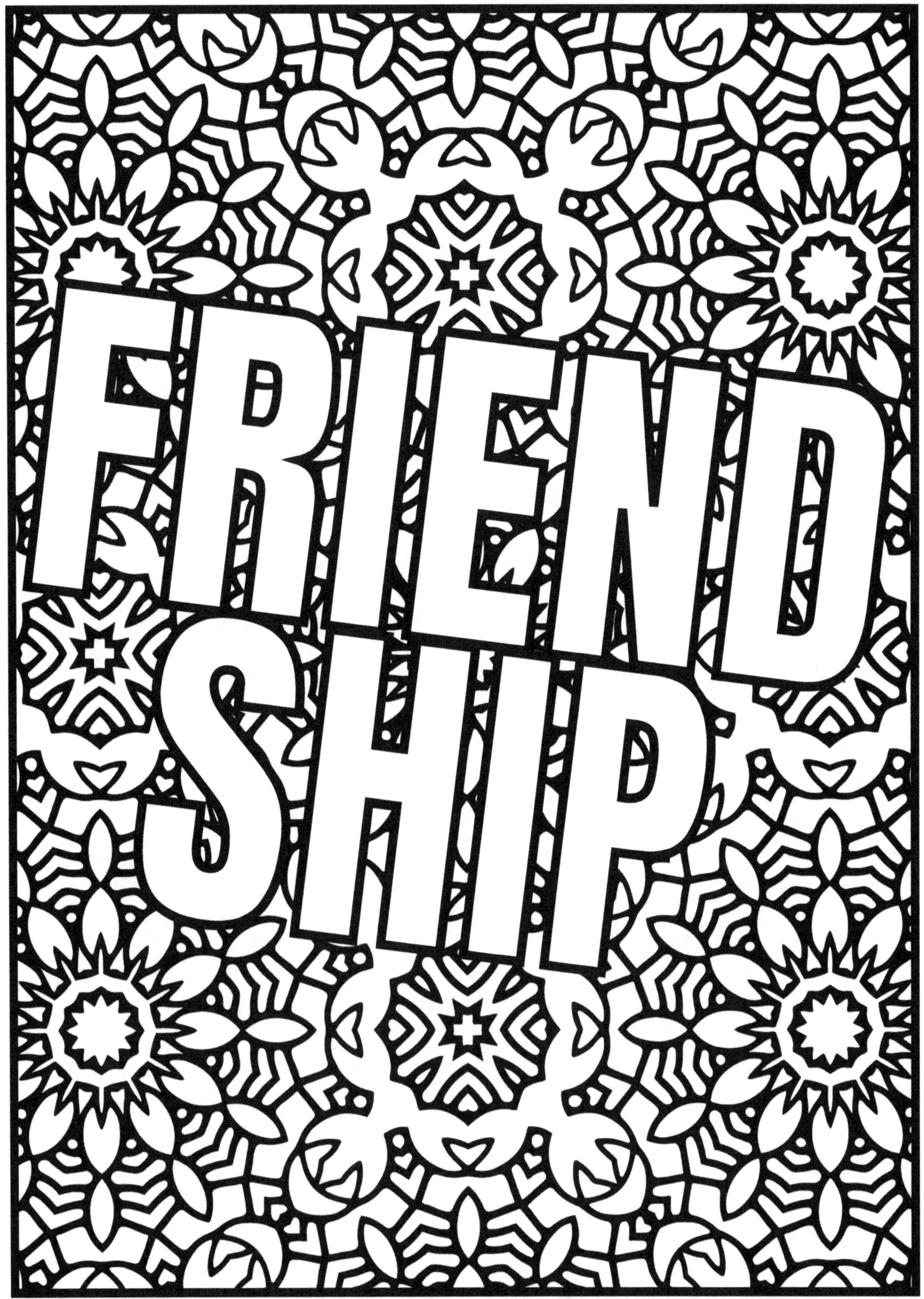
FRIEND
SHIP

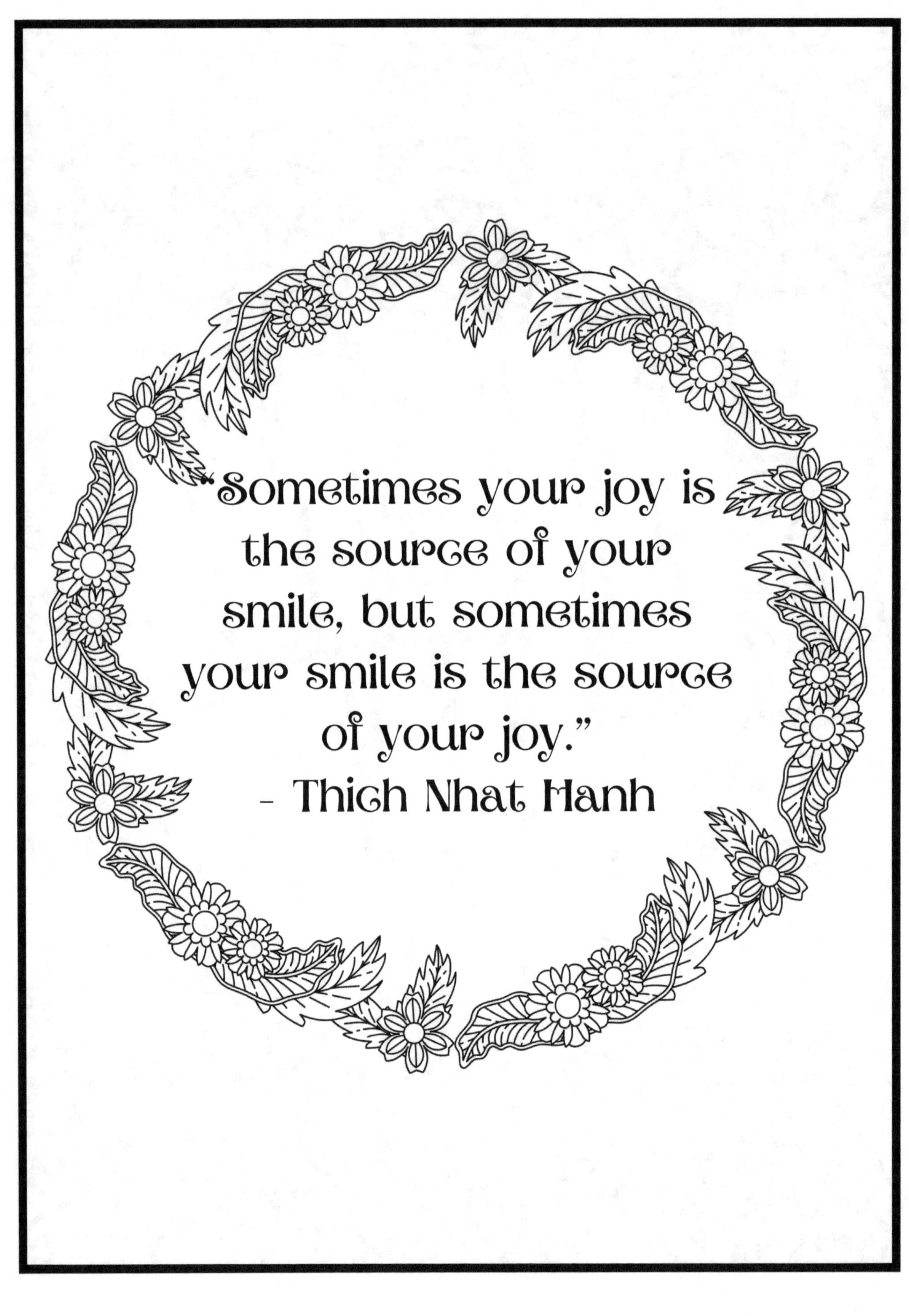
"Sometimes your joy is
the source of your
smile, but sometimes
your smile is the source
of your joy."
- Thich Nhat Hanh

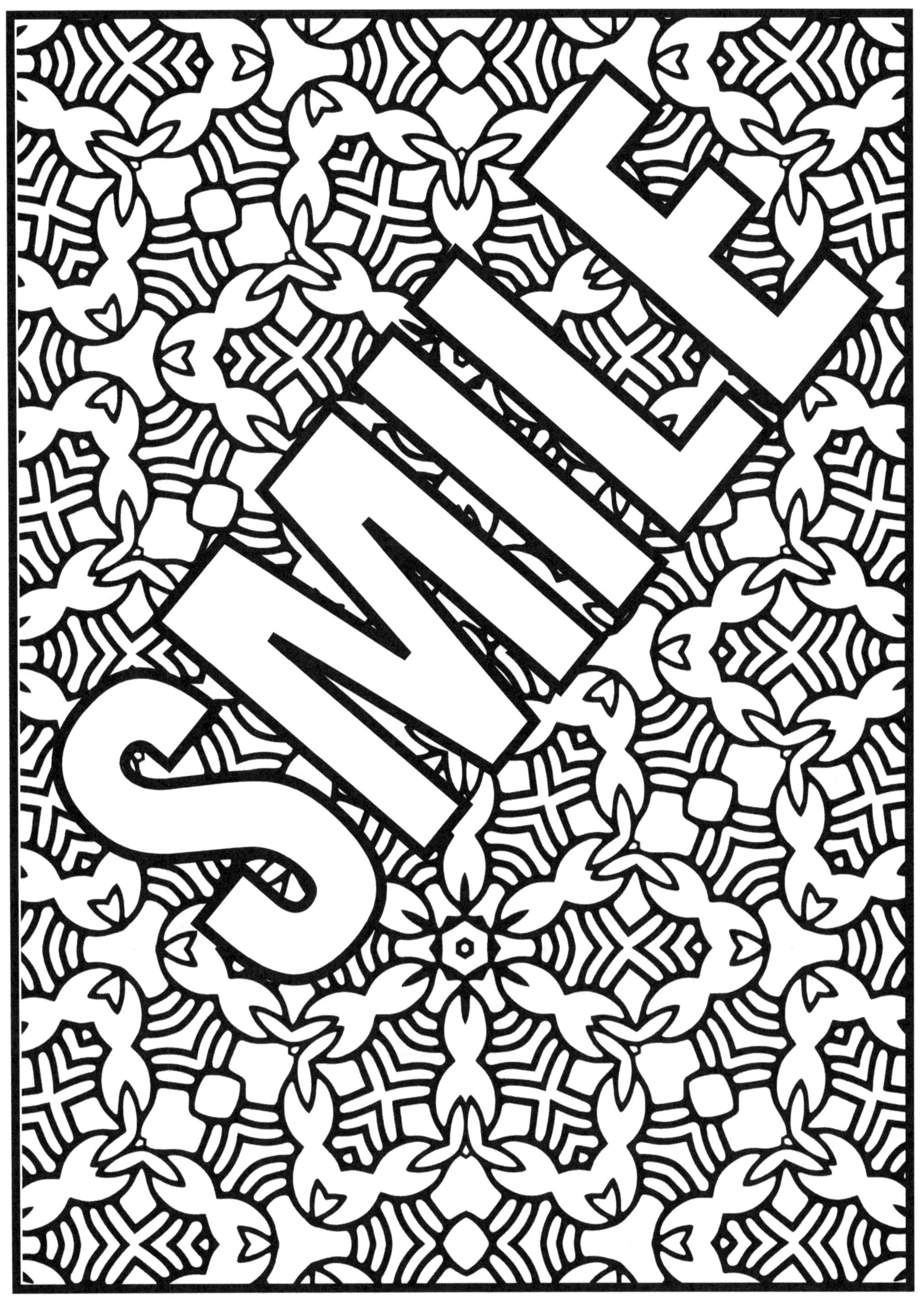
SMILE

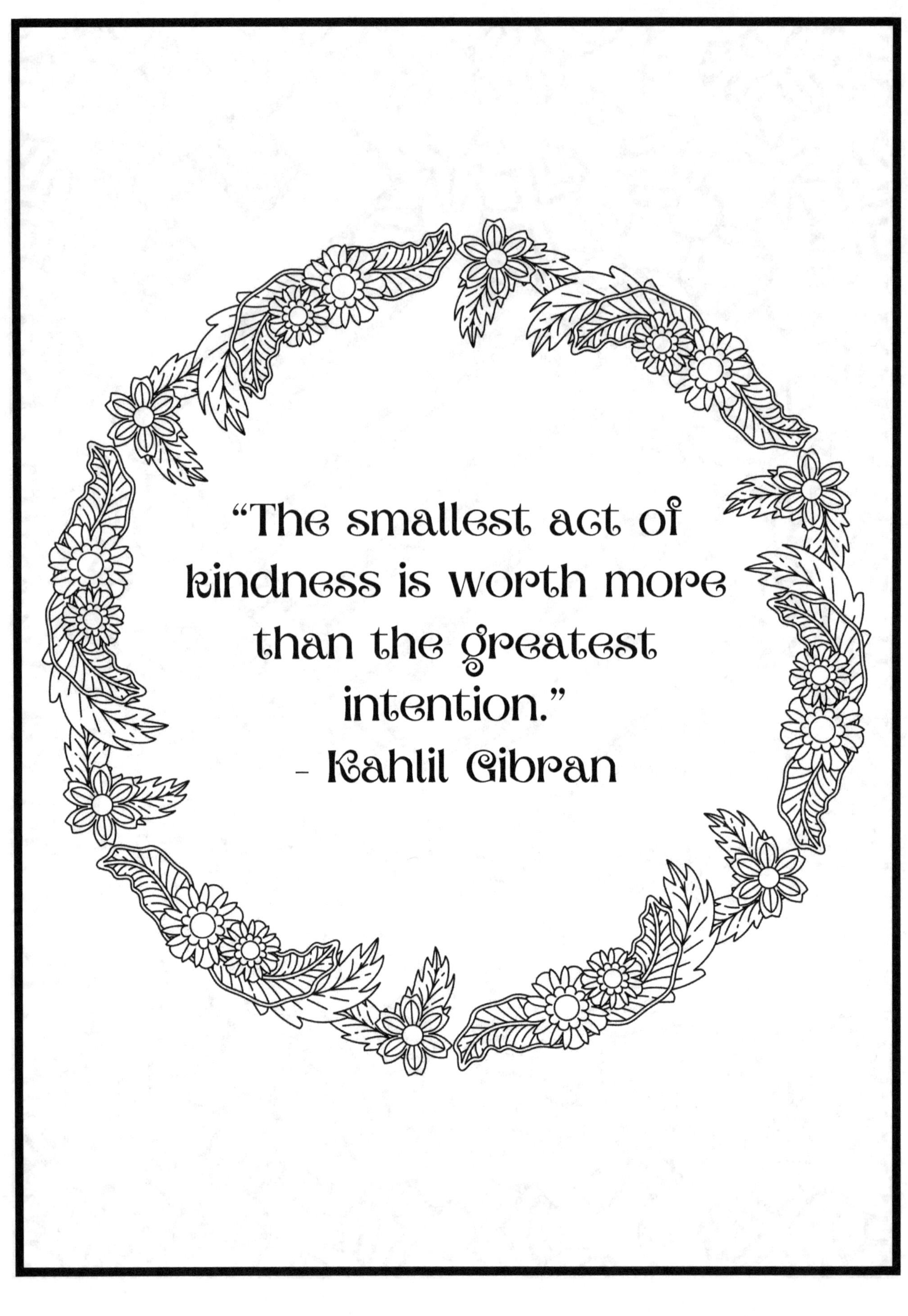
"The smallest act of
kindness is worth more
than the greatest
intention."
- Kahlil Gibran

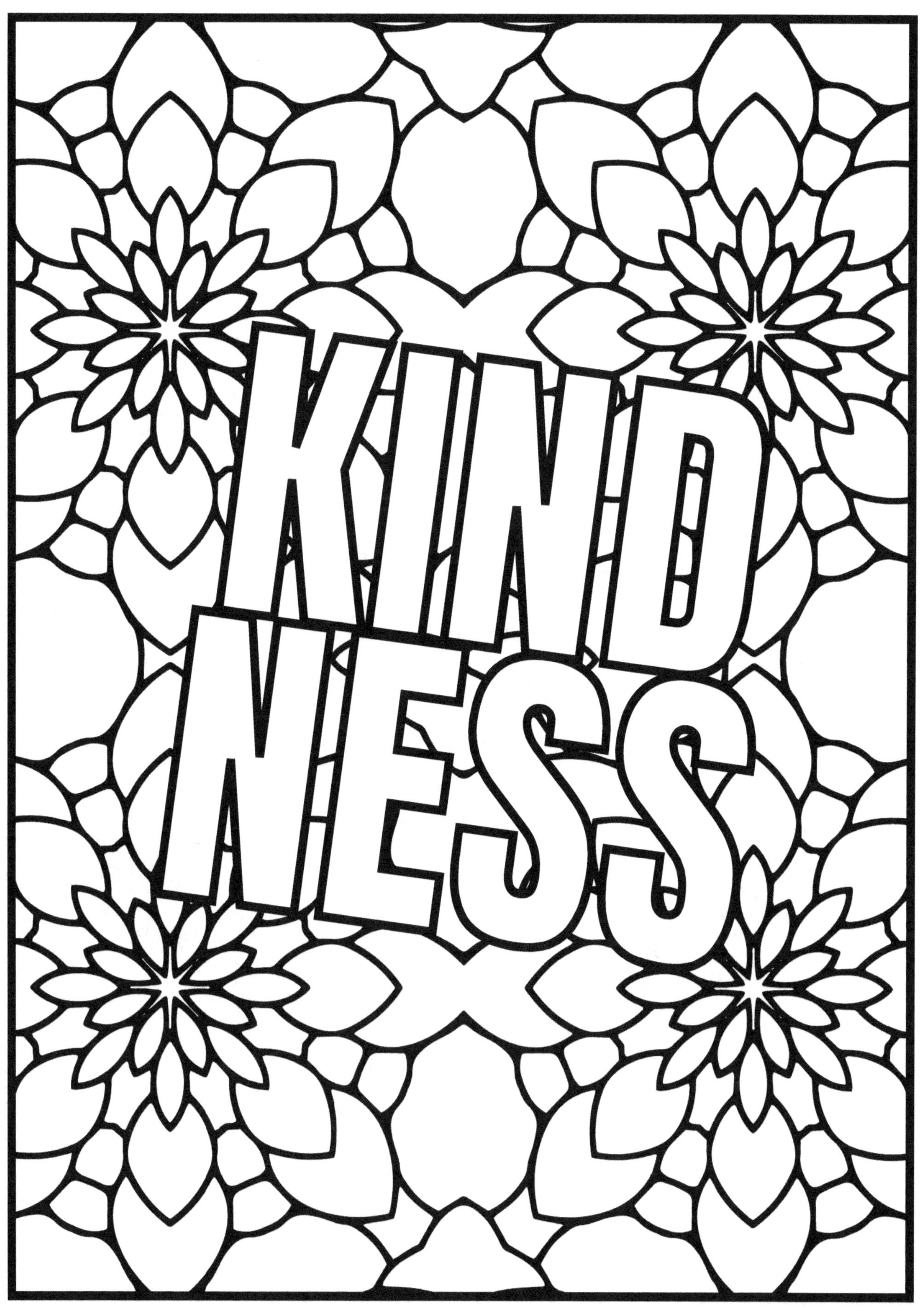
KIND
NESS

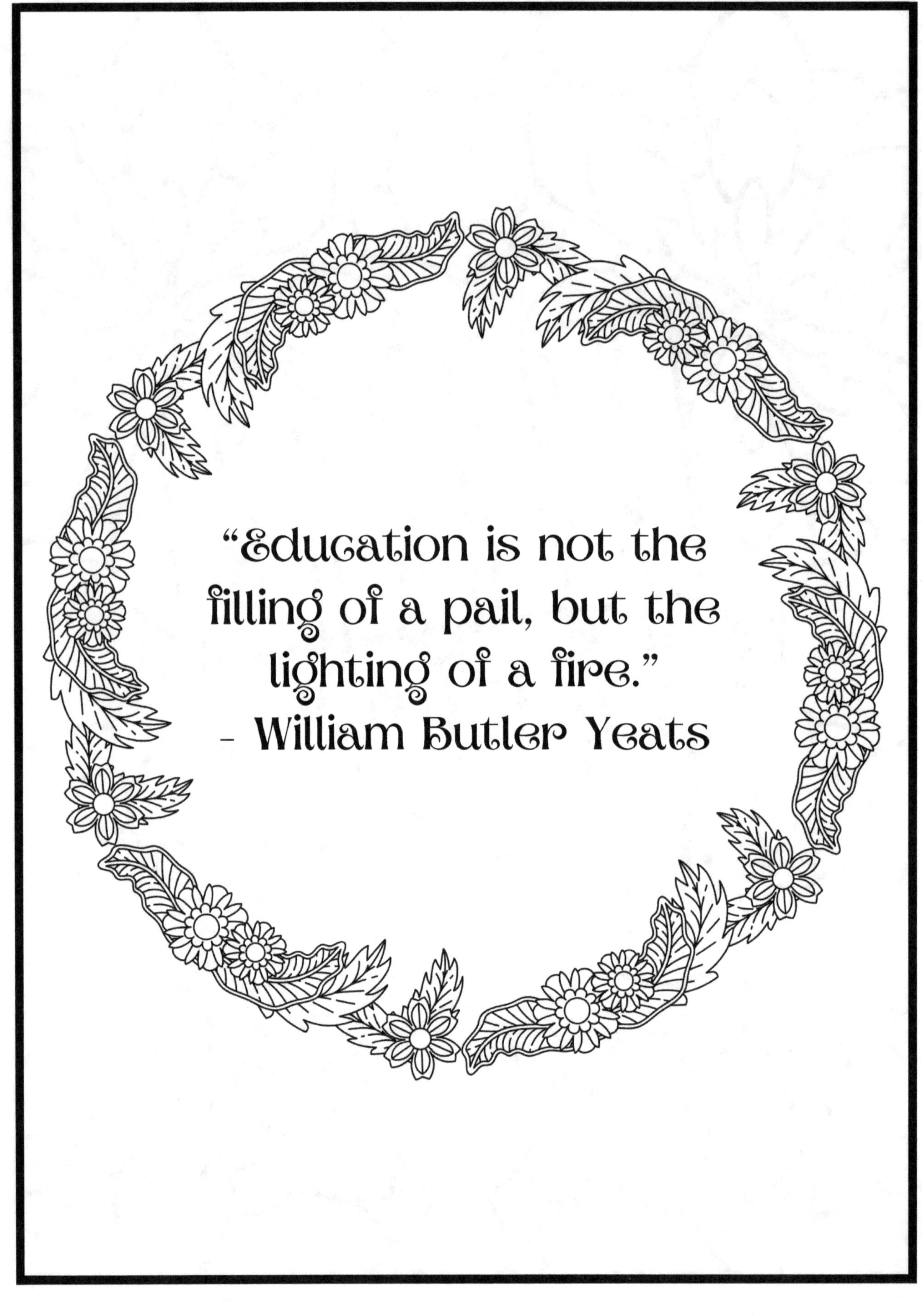
"Education is not the filling of a pail, but the lighting of a fire."
- William Butler Yeats

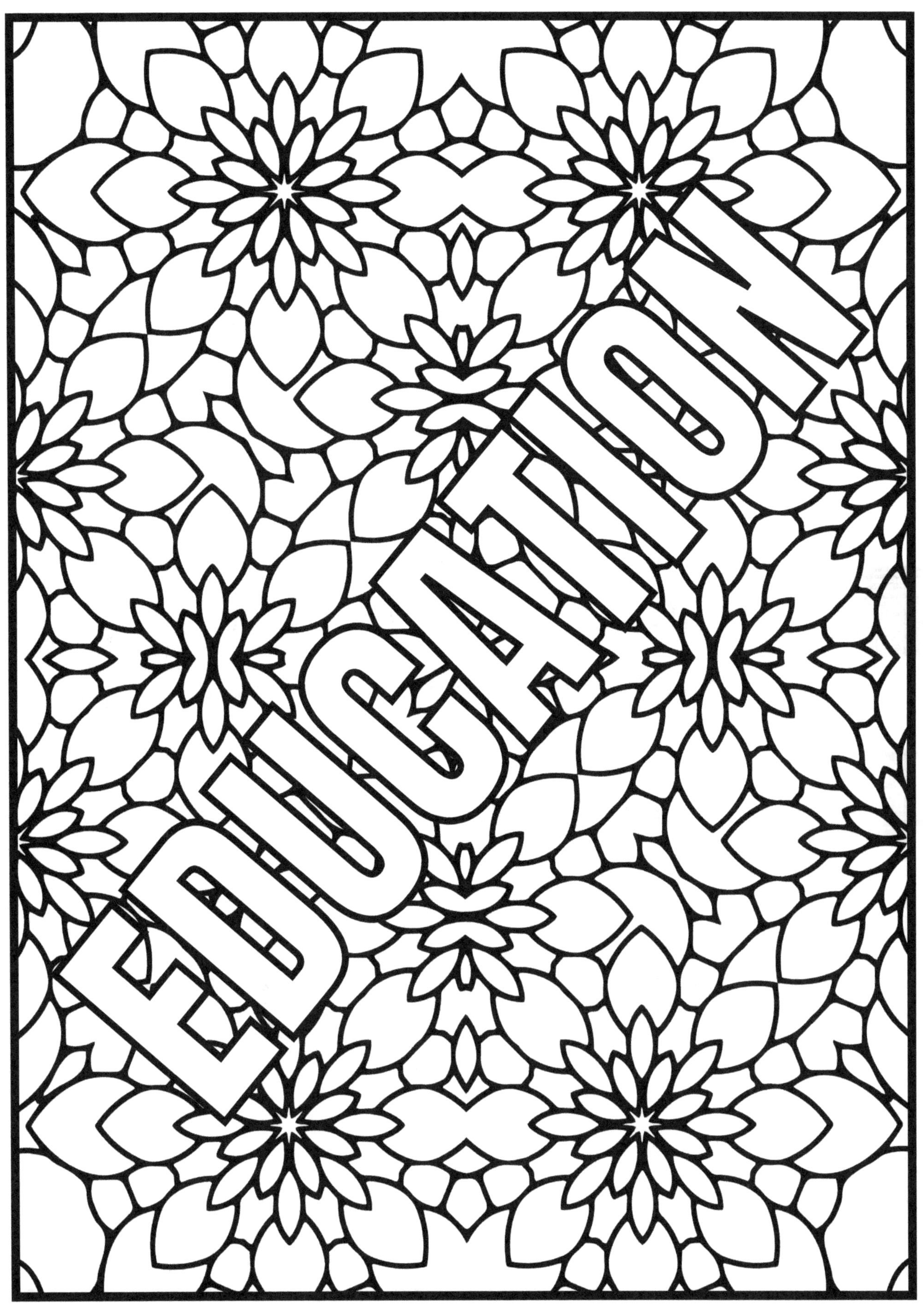
EDUCATION

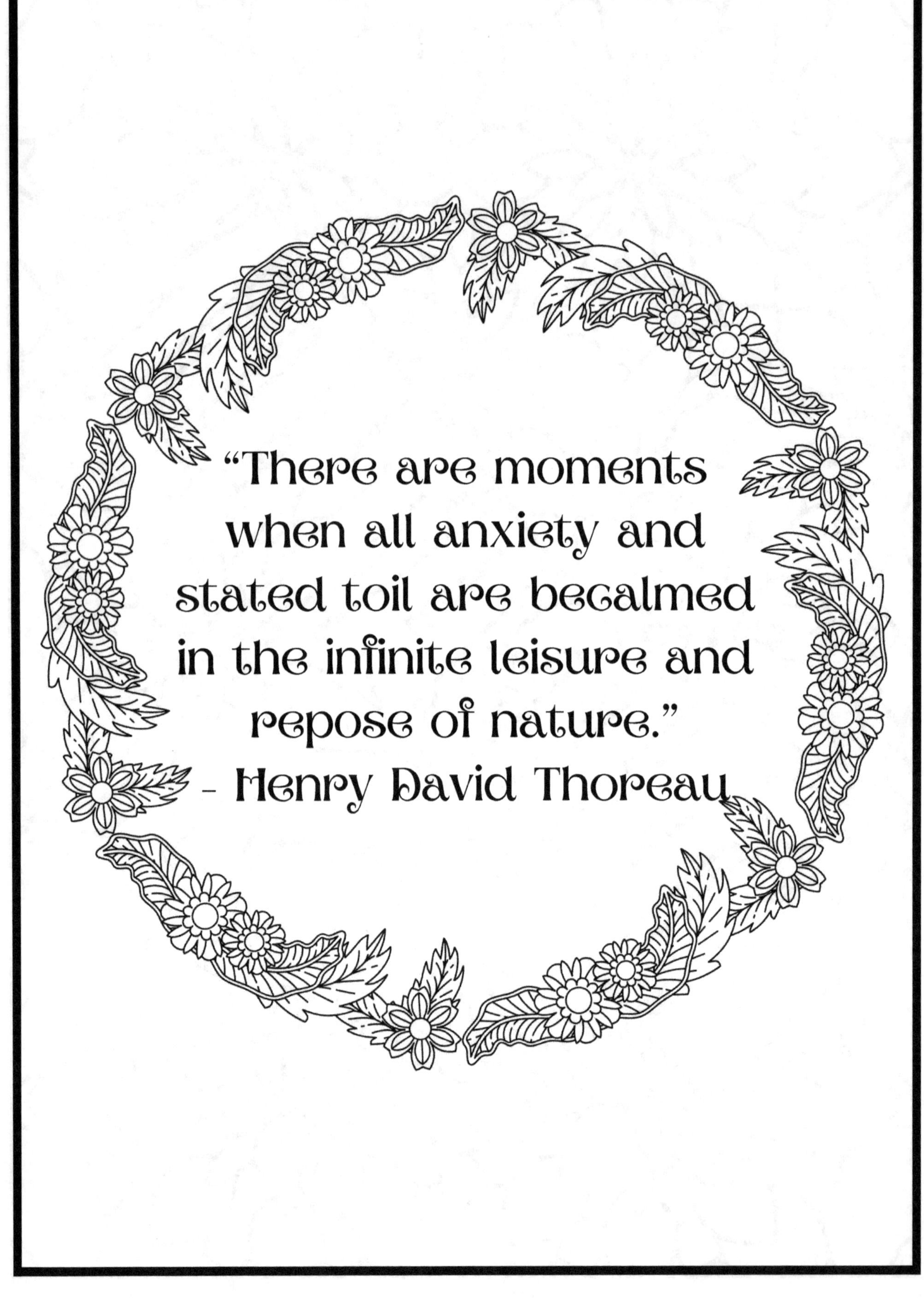
"There are moments
when all anxiety and
stated toil are becalmed
in the infinite leisure and
repose of nature."
- Henry David Thoreau

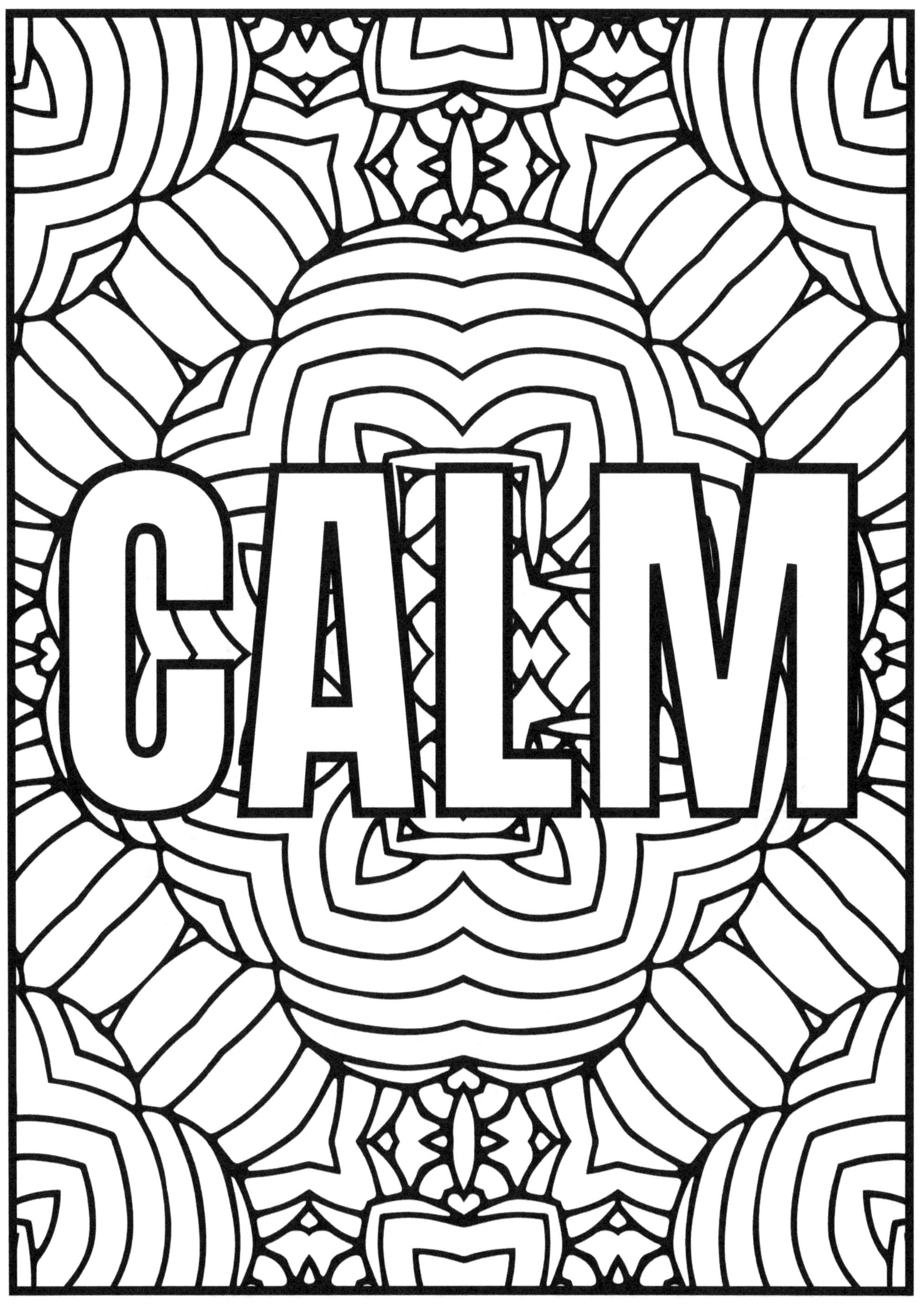
CALM

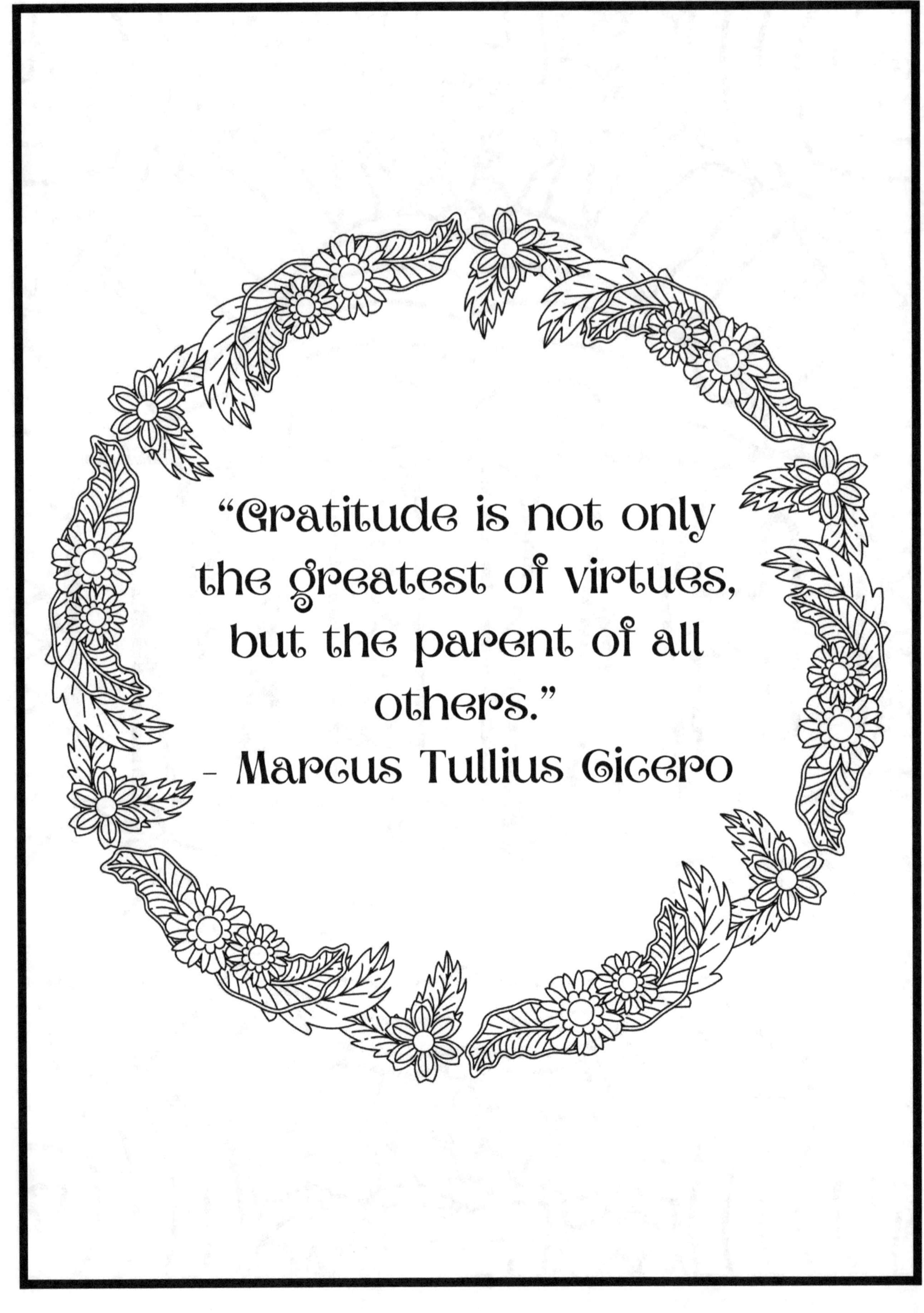
"Gratitude is not only
the greatest of virtues,
but the parent of all
others."
- Marcus Tullius Cicero

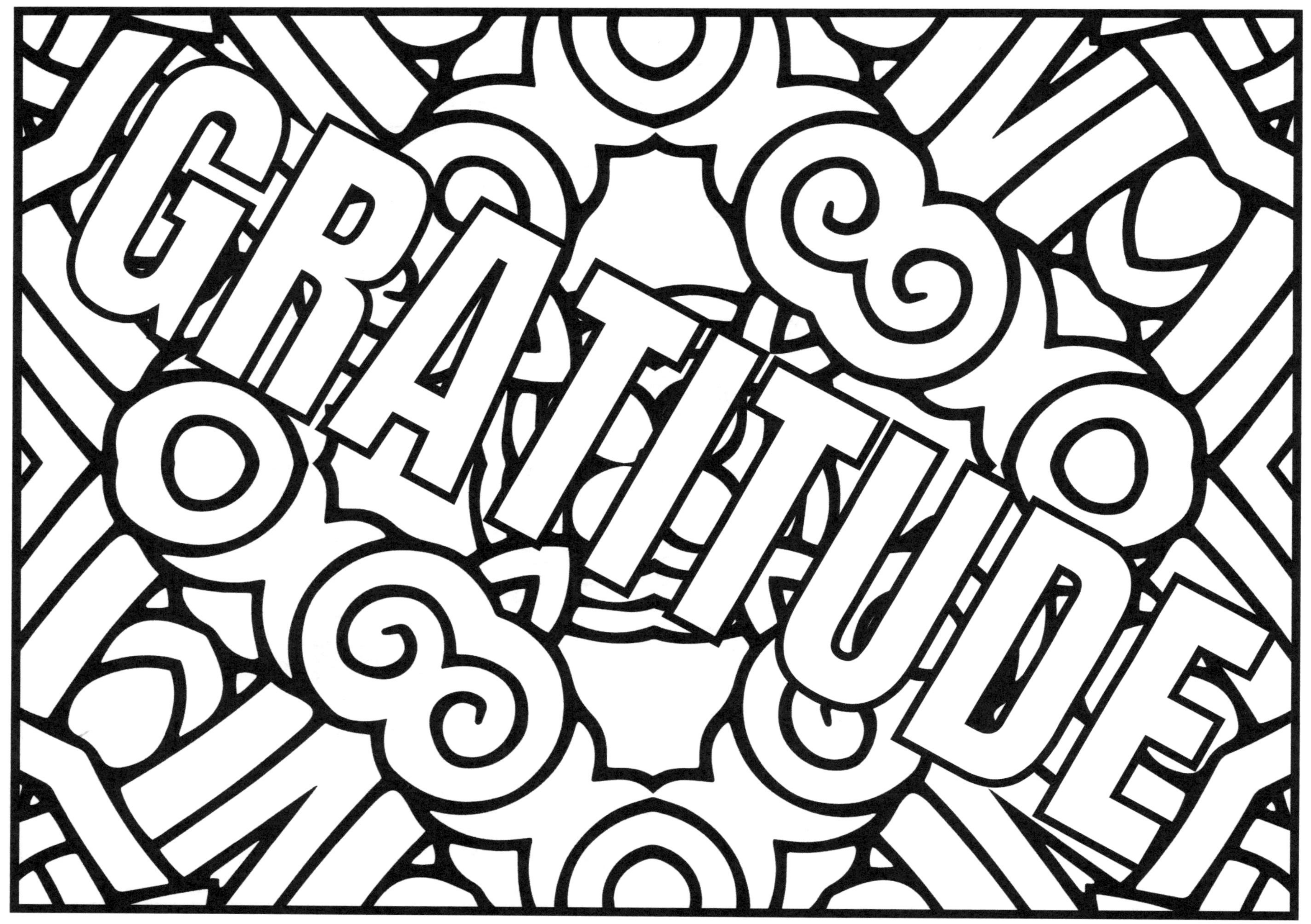
GRATITUDE

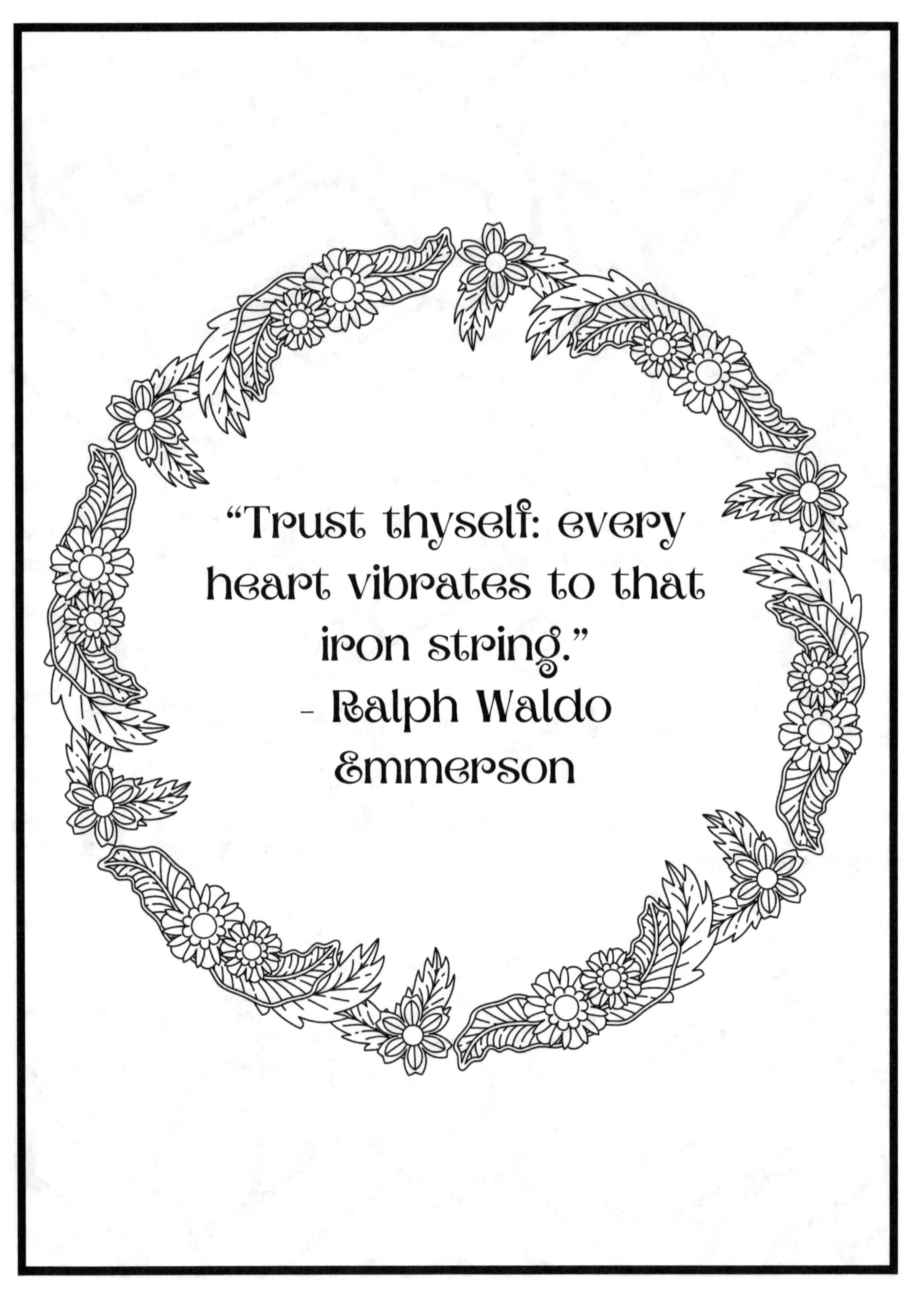
"Trust thyself: every
heart vibrates to that
iron string."
- Ralph Waldo
Emmerson

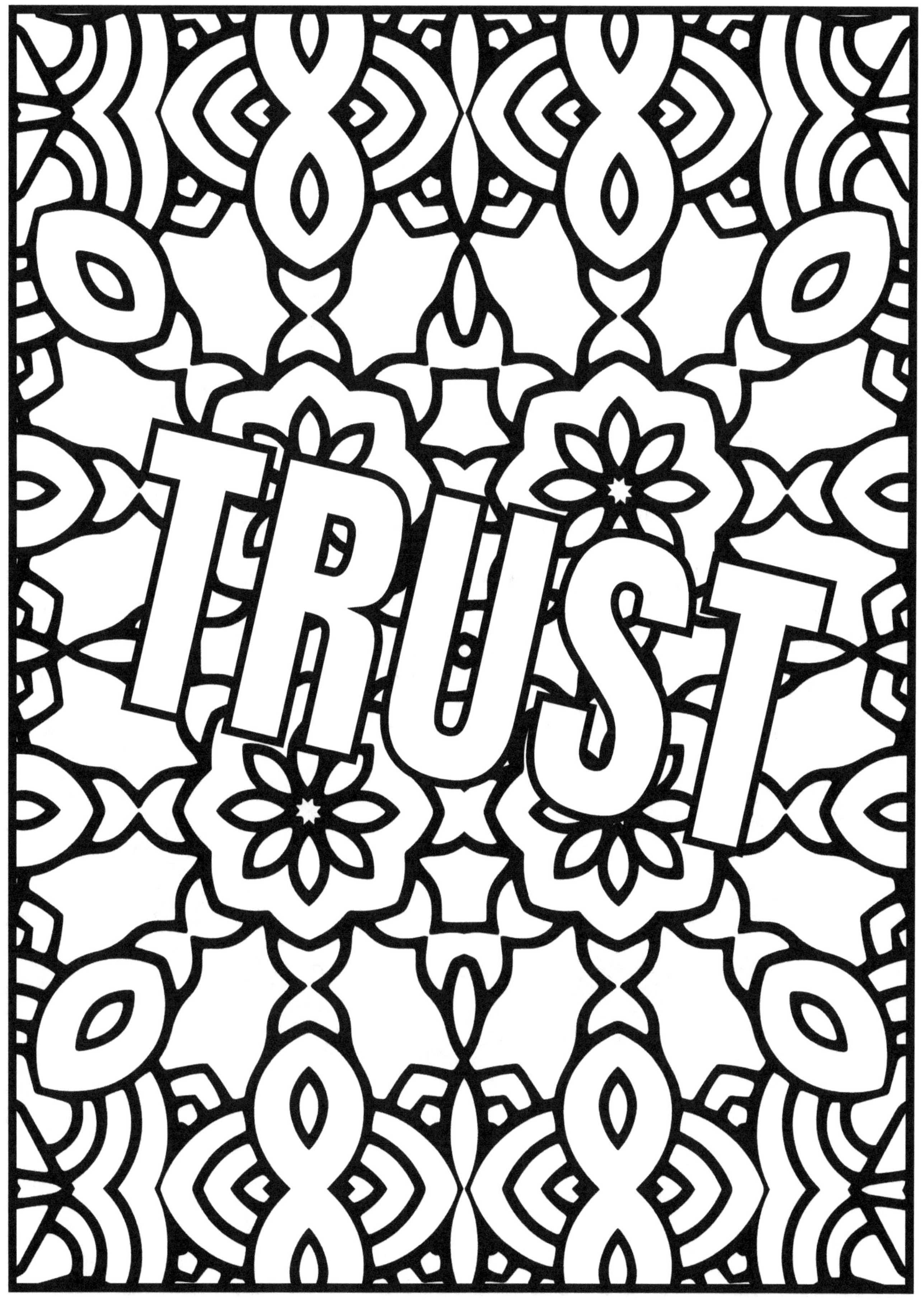
TRUST

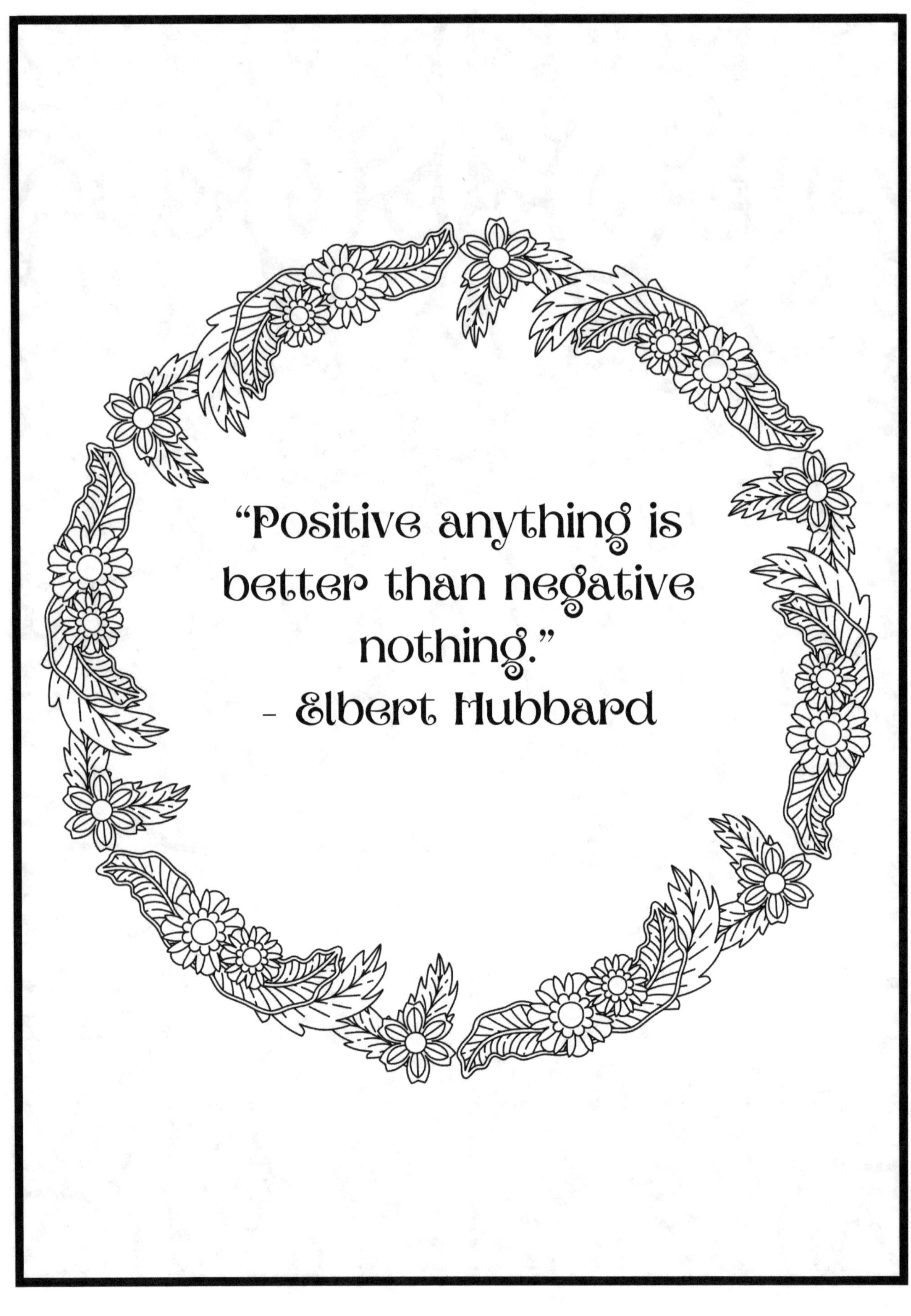
"Positive anything is
better than negative
nothing."
- Elbert Hubbard

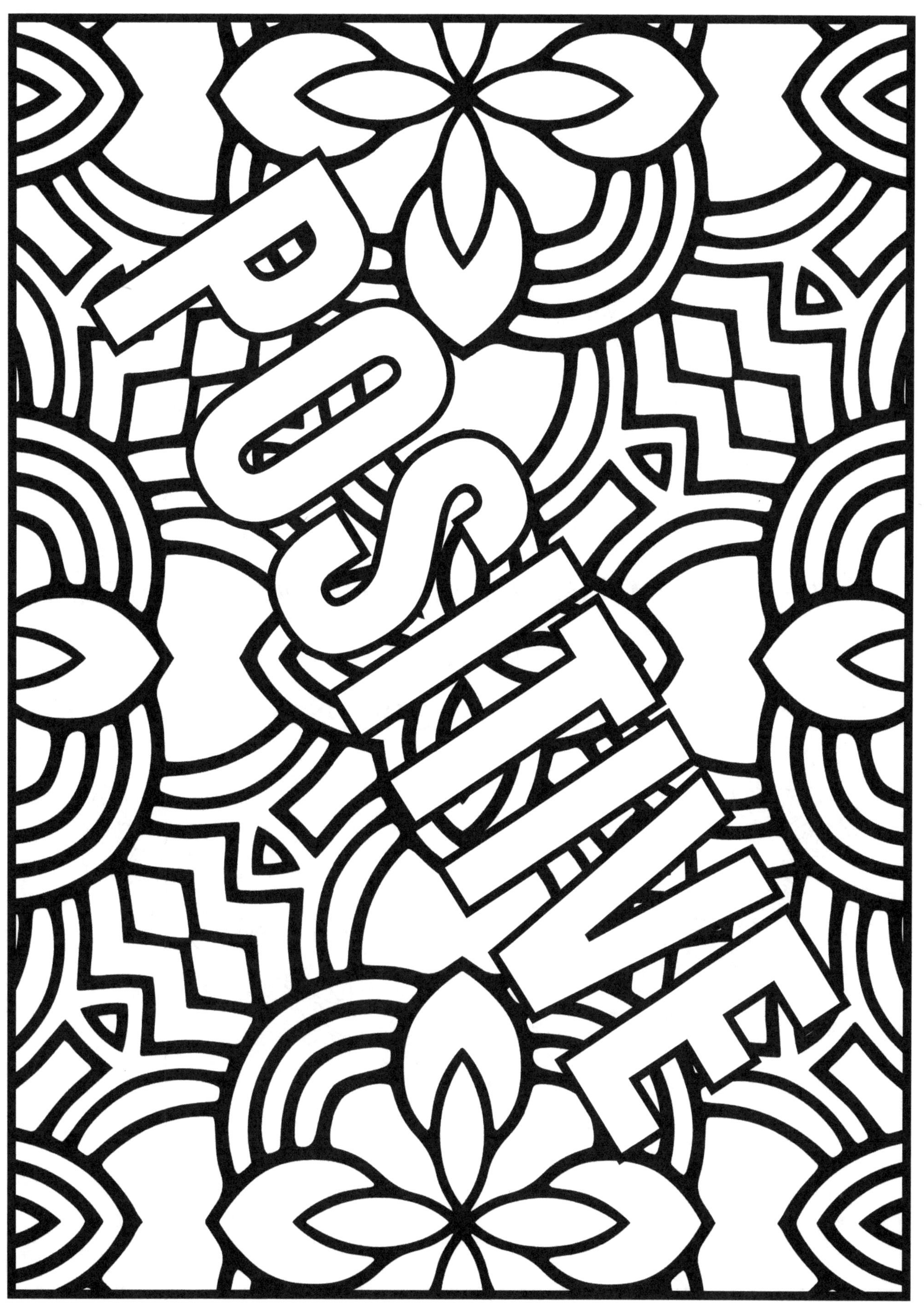
POSITIVE

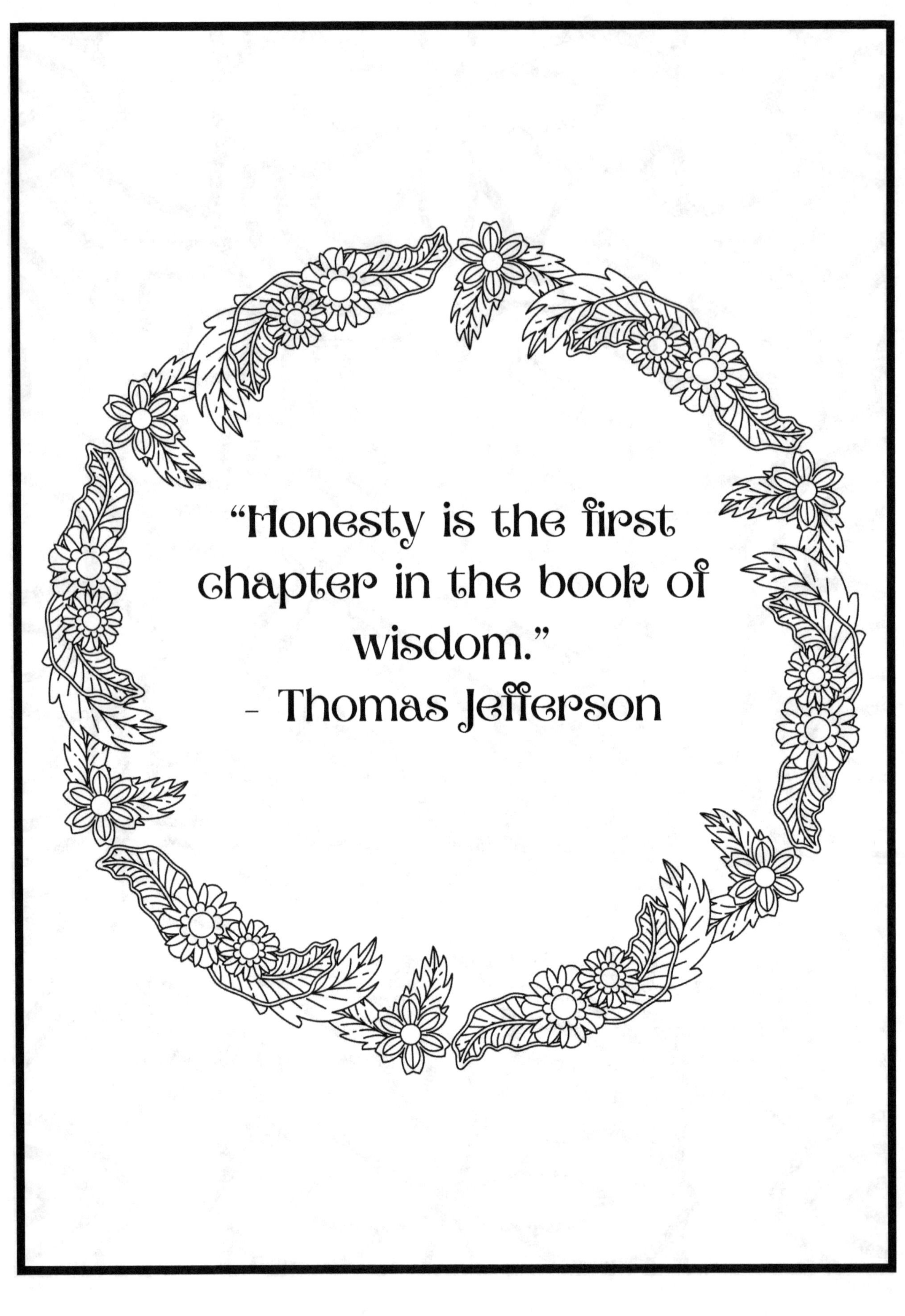
"Honesty is the first chapter in the book of wisdom."
- Thomas Jefferson

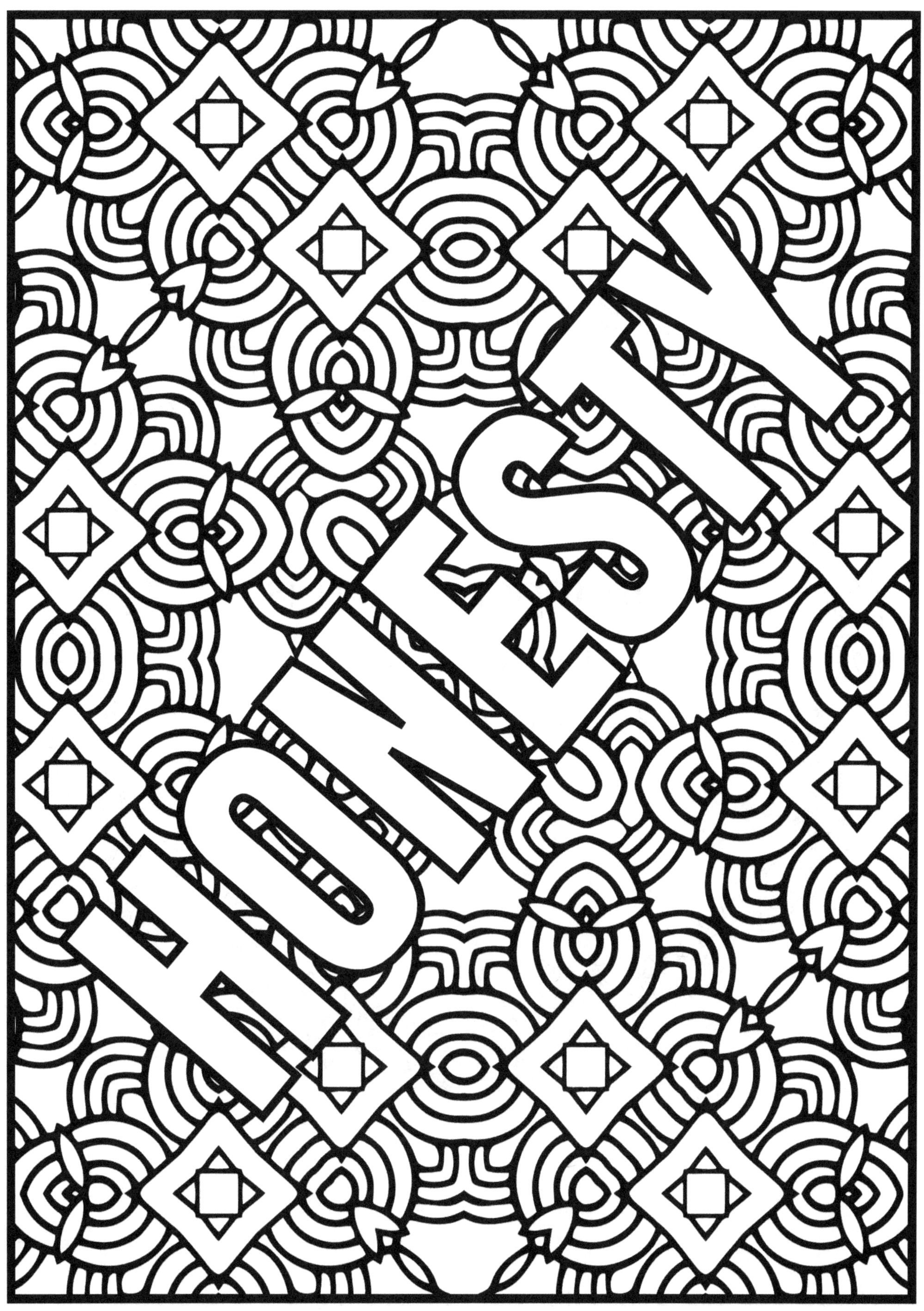
HONESTY

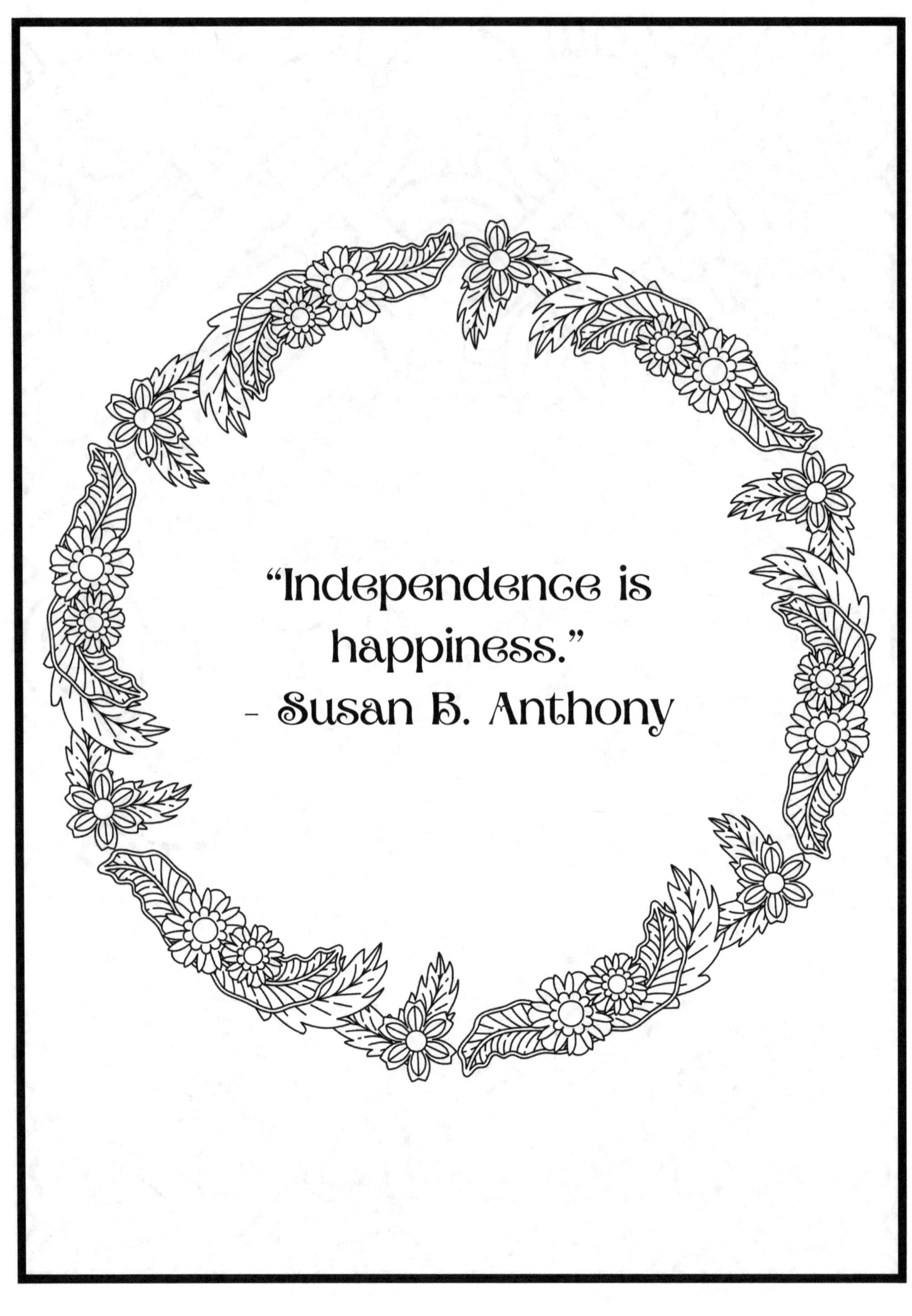
“Independence is
happiness.”
- Susan B. Anthony

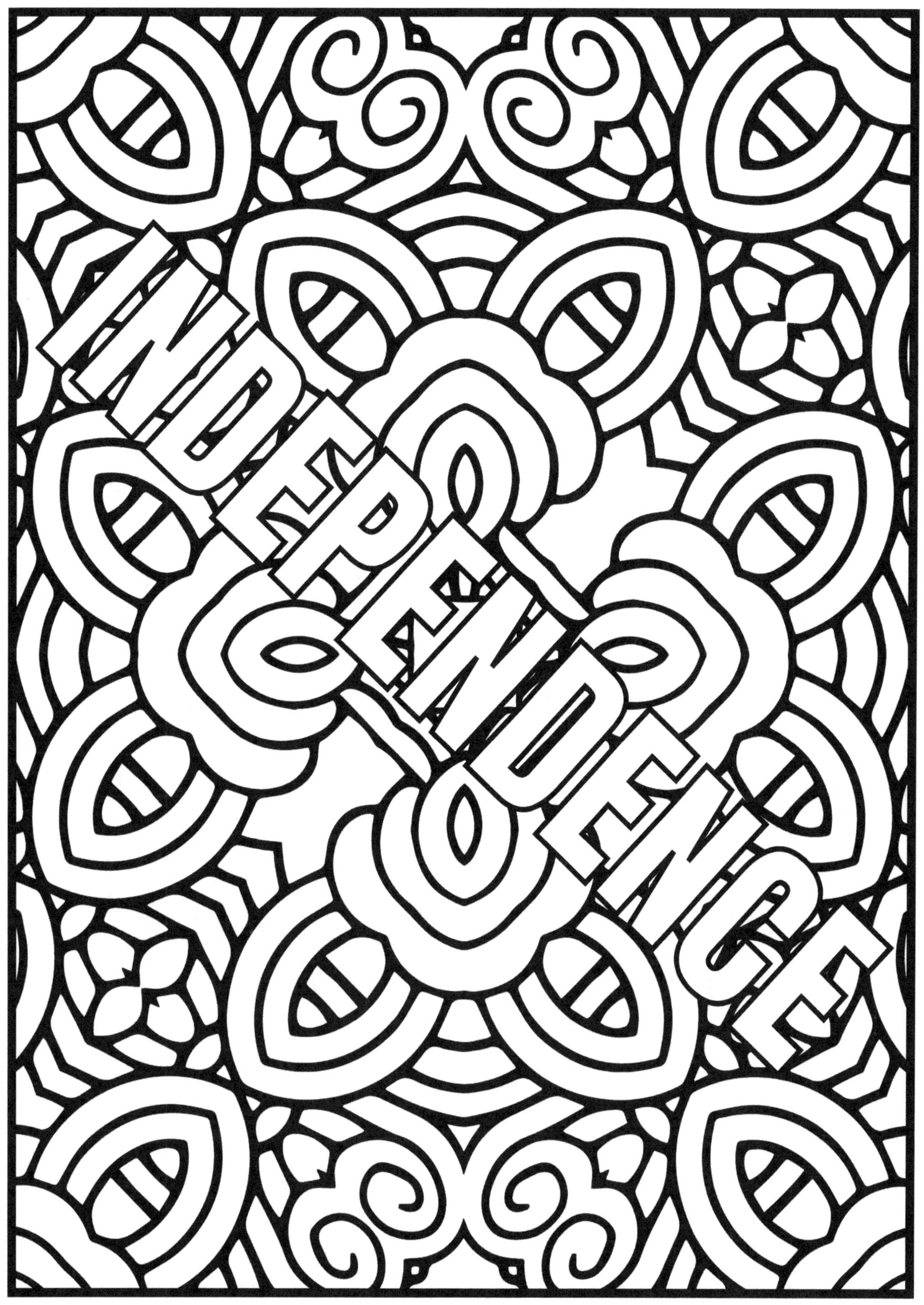
INDEPENDENCE

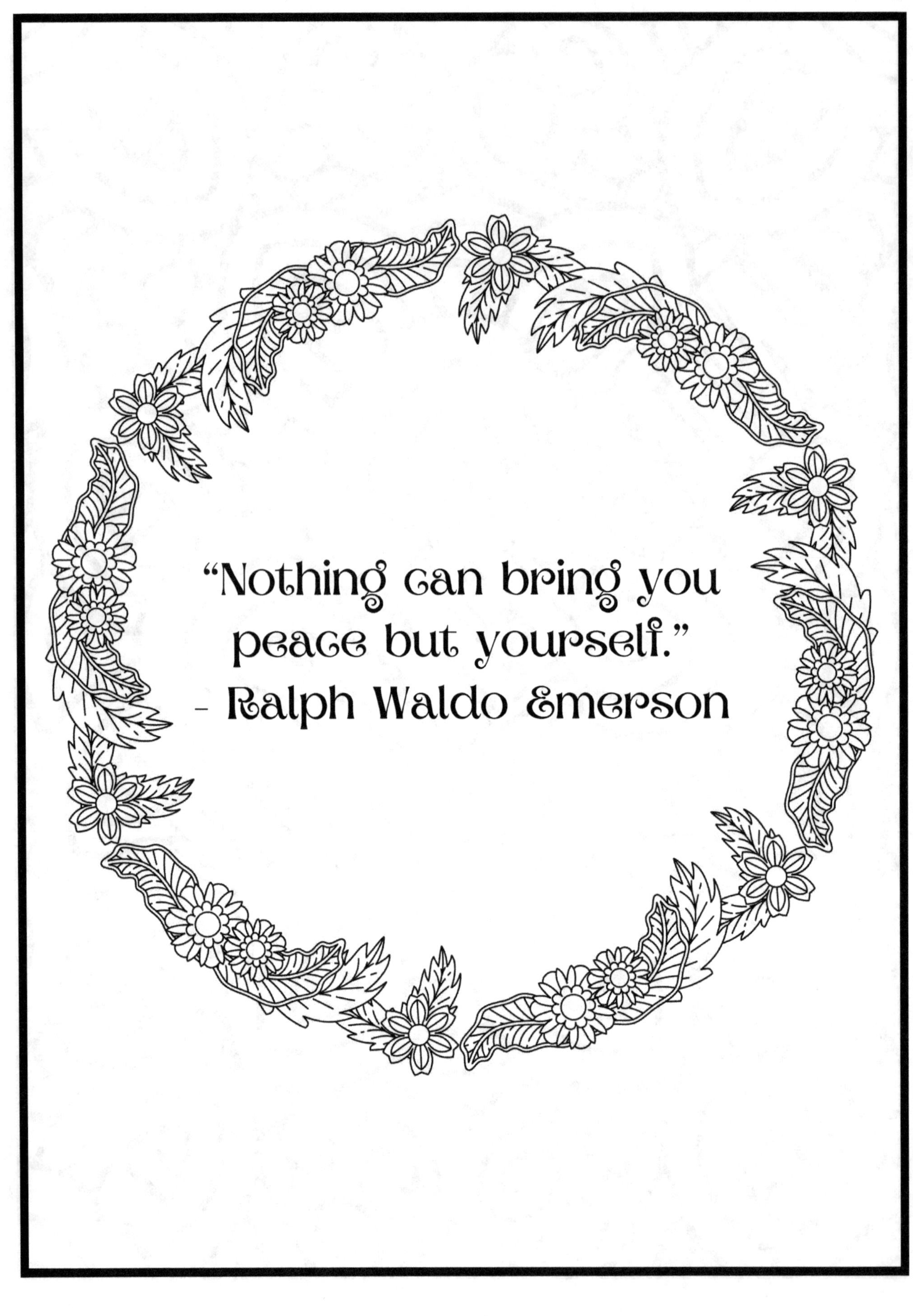
"Nothing can bring you
peace but yourself."
- Ralph Waldo Emerson

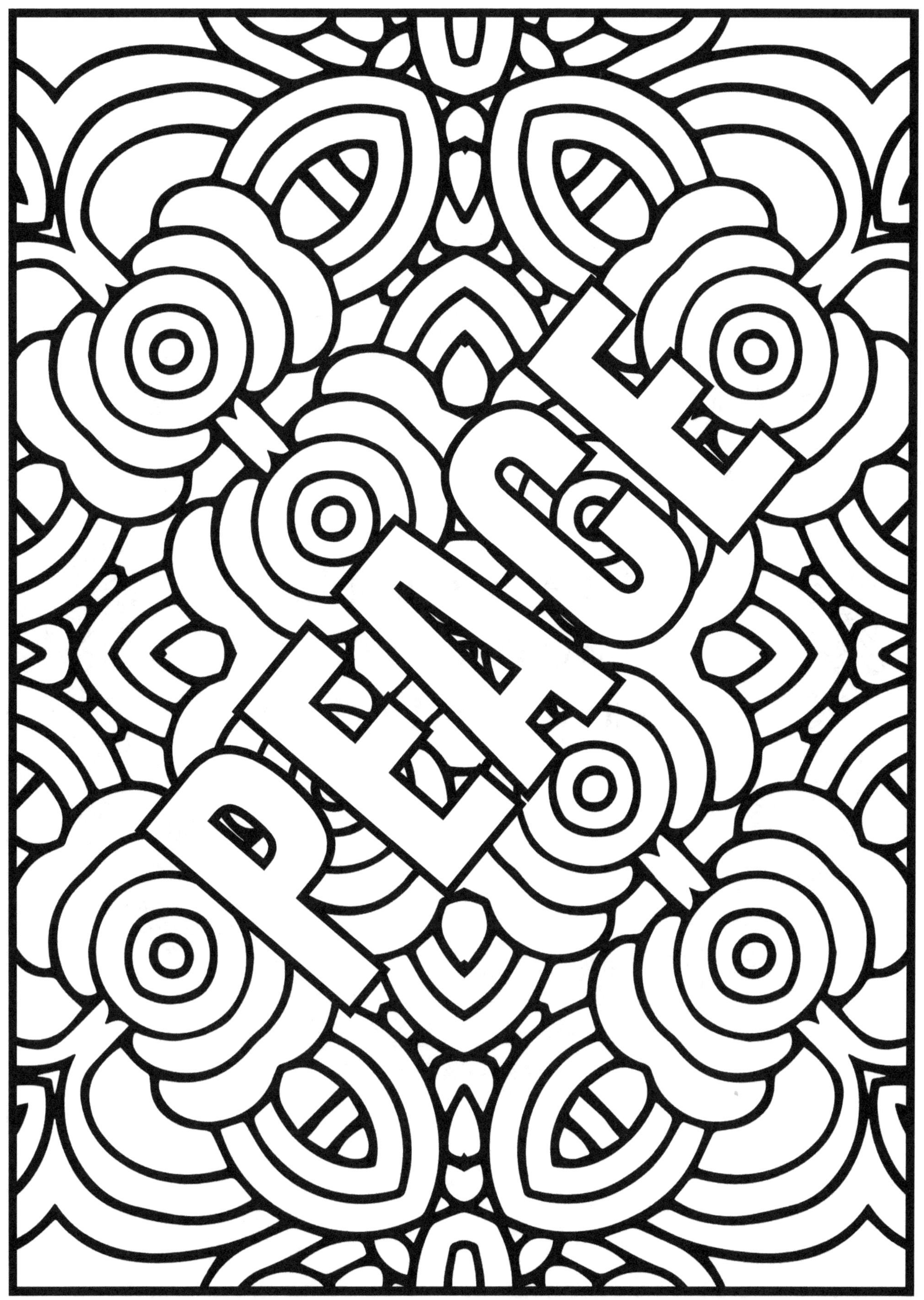
PEACE

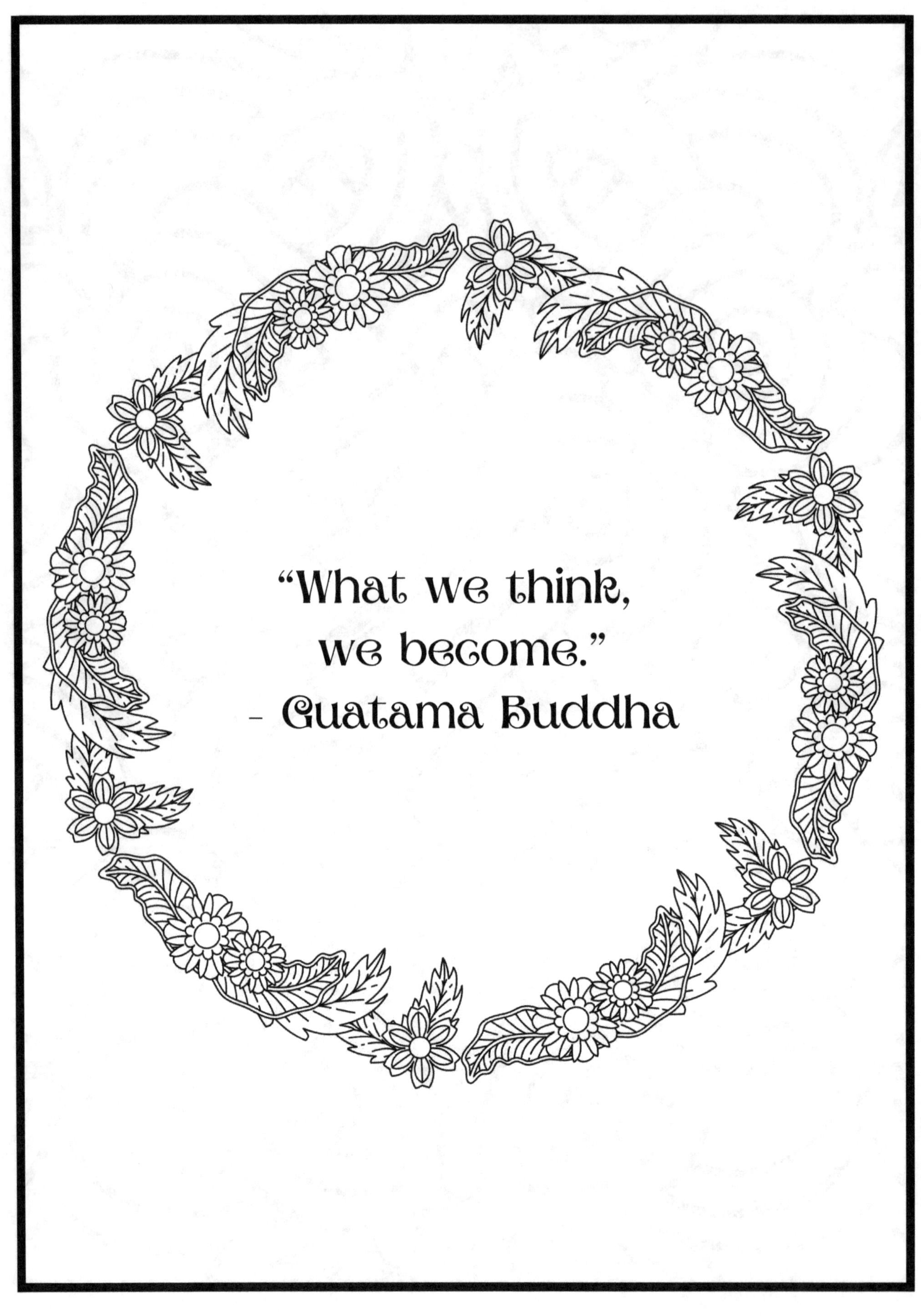
"What we think,
we become."
- Guatama Buddha

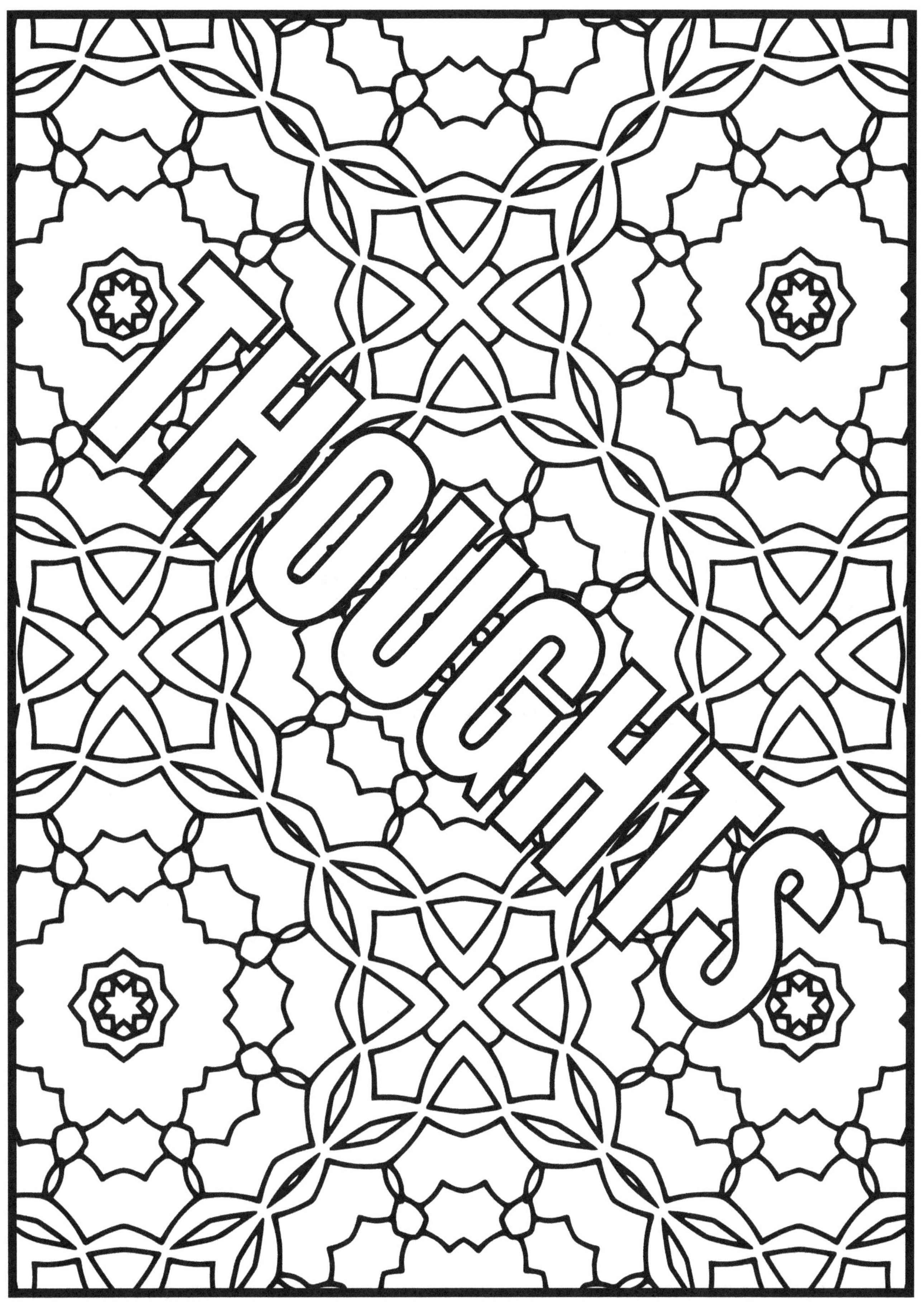
THOUGHTS

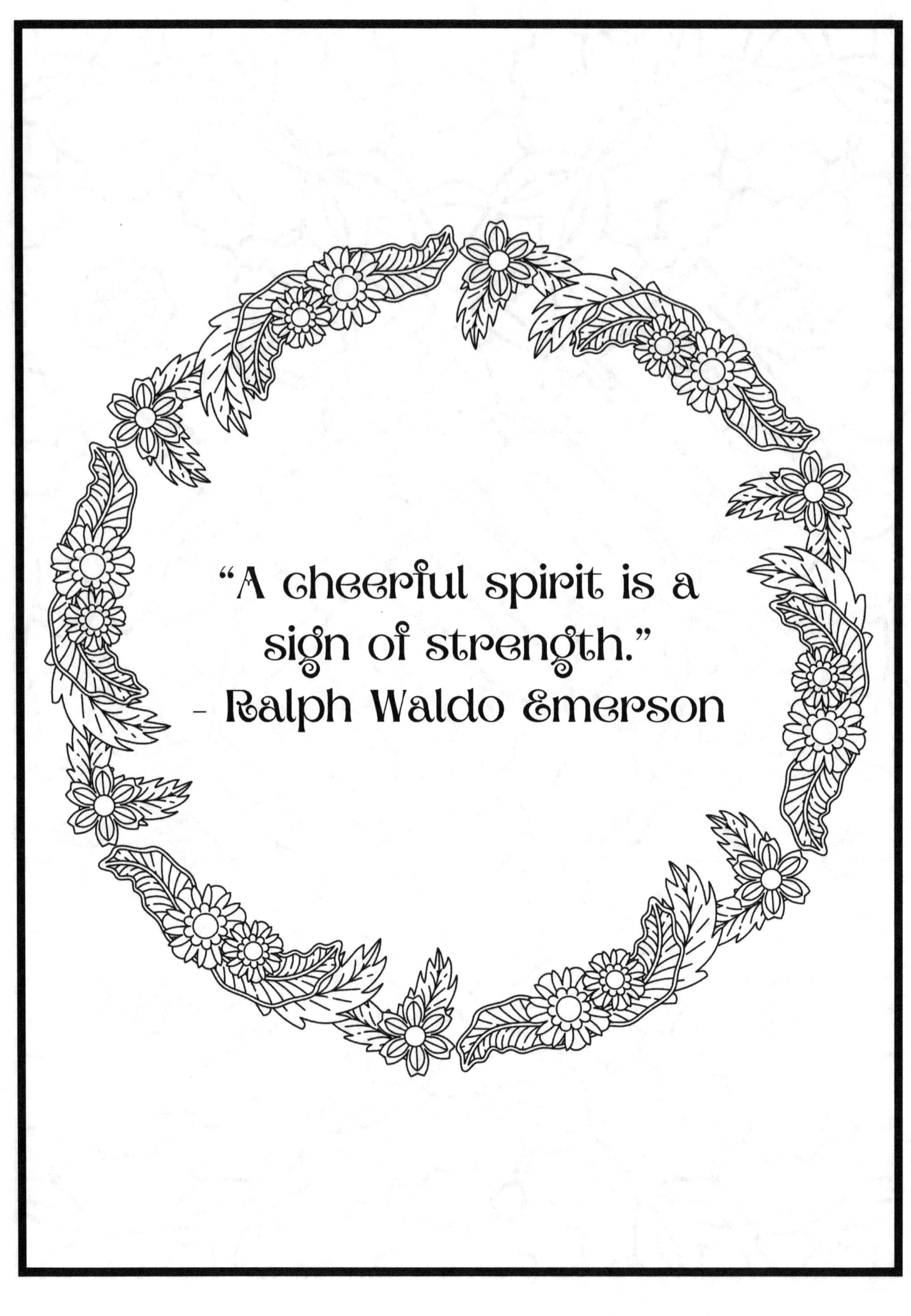
"A cheerful spirit is a
sign of strength."
- Ralph Waldo Emerson

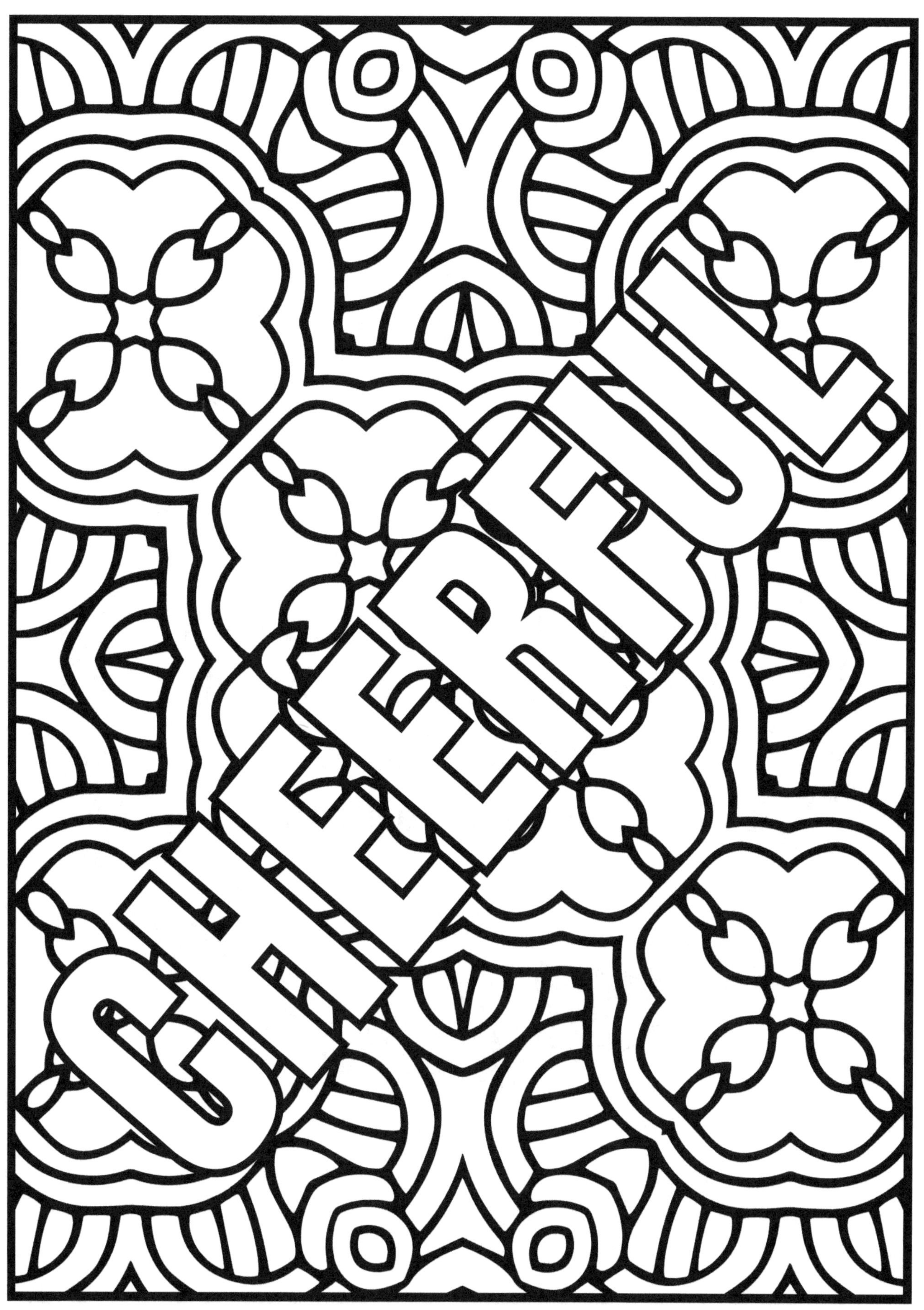
CHEERFUL

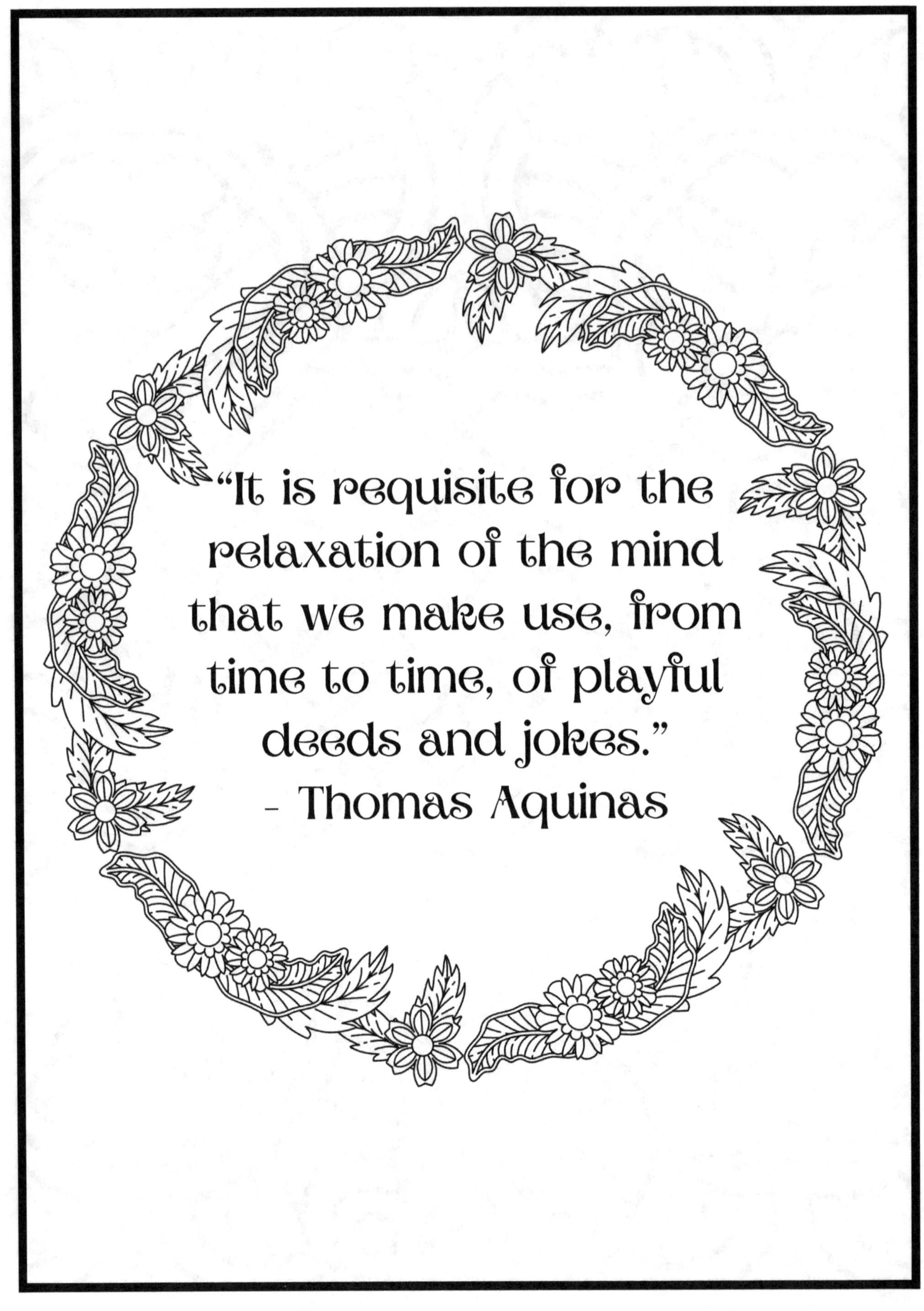
"It is requisite for the
relaxation of the mind
that we make use, from
time to time, of playful
deeds and jokes."
- Thomas Aquinas

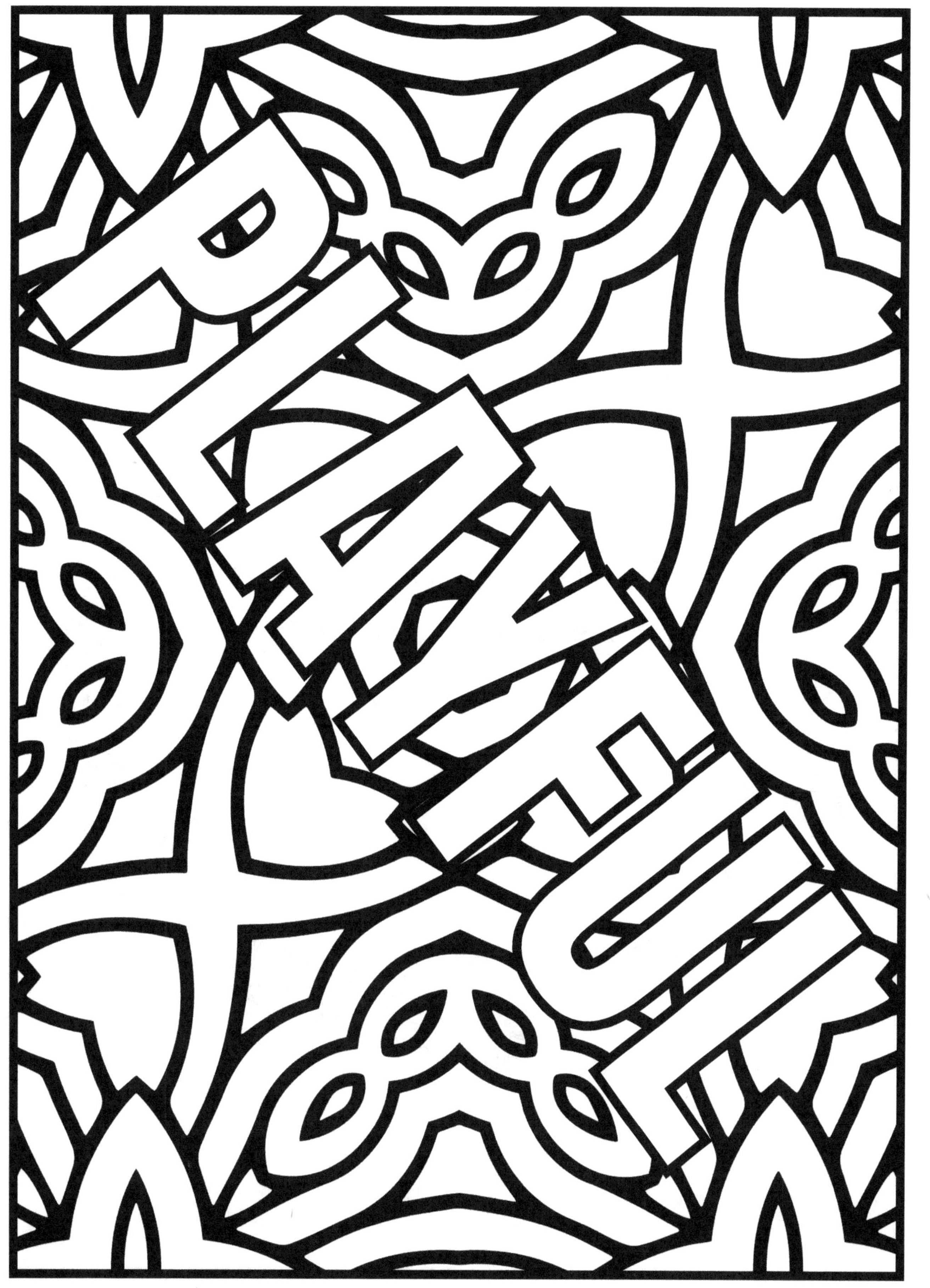
PLAYFUL

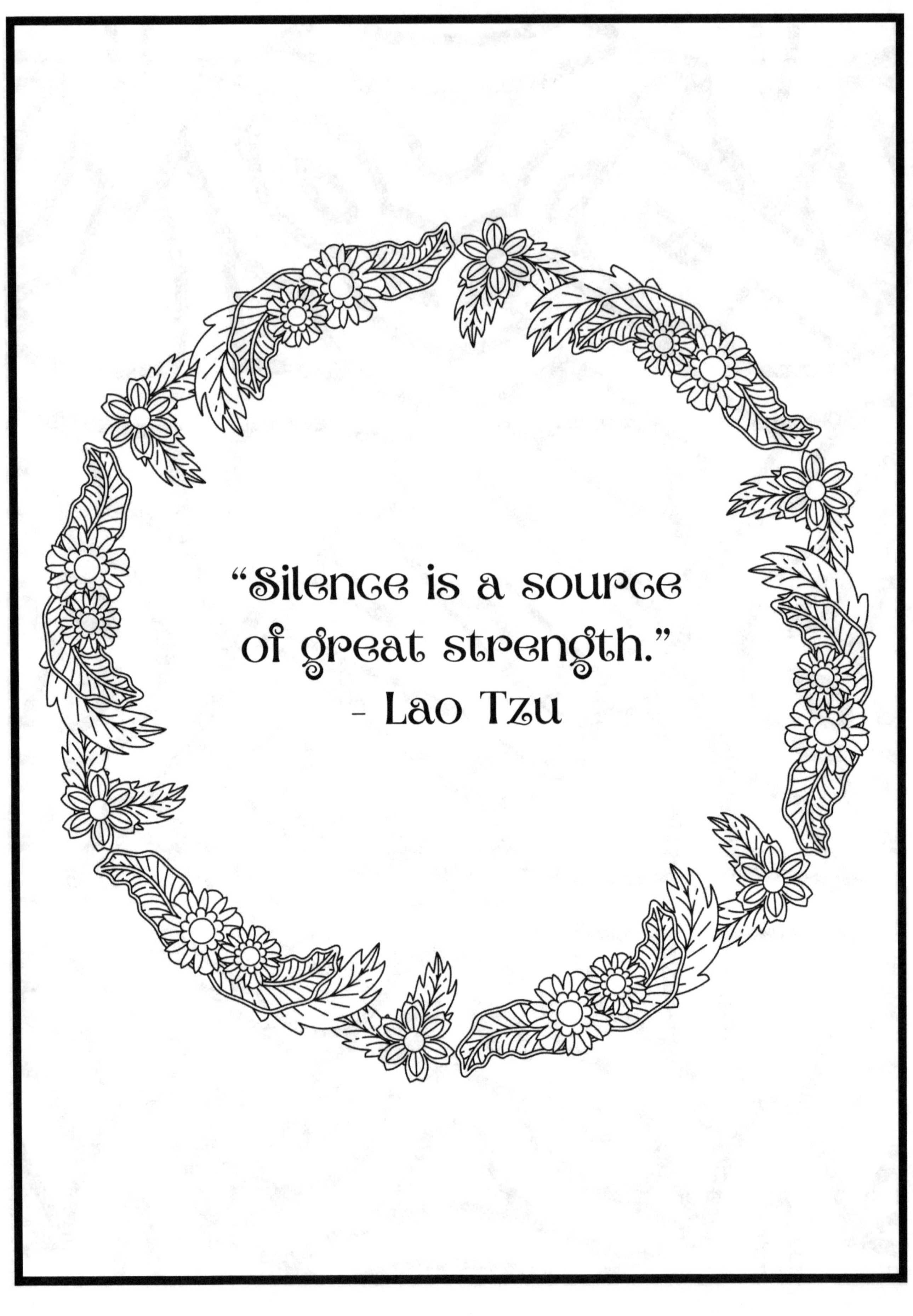
"Silence is a source
of great strength."
- Lao Tzu

SILENCE

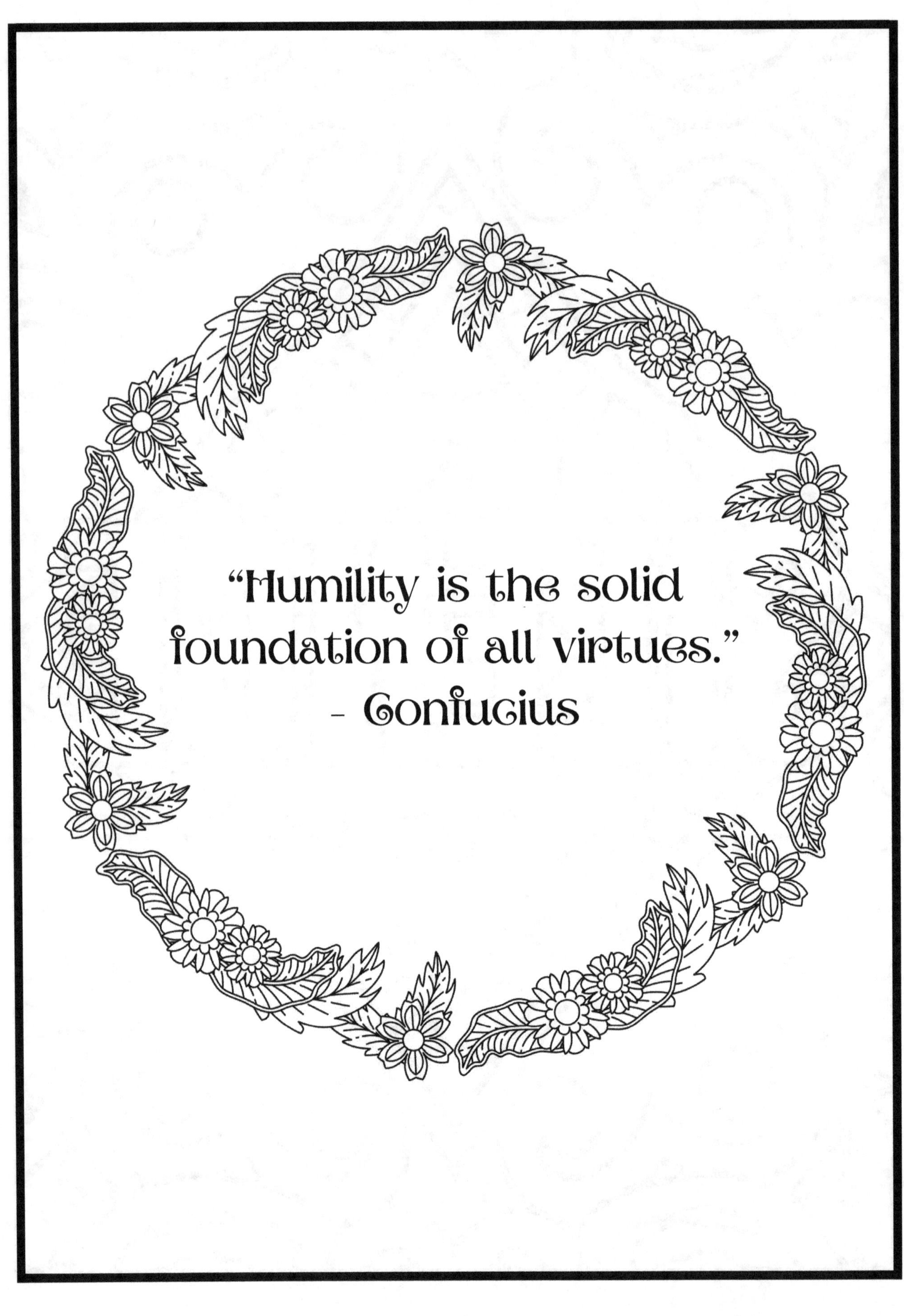
"Humility is the solid
foundation of all virtues."
- Confucius

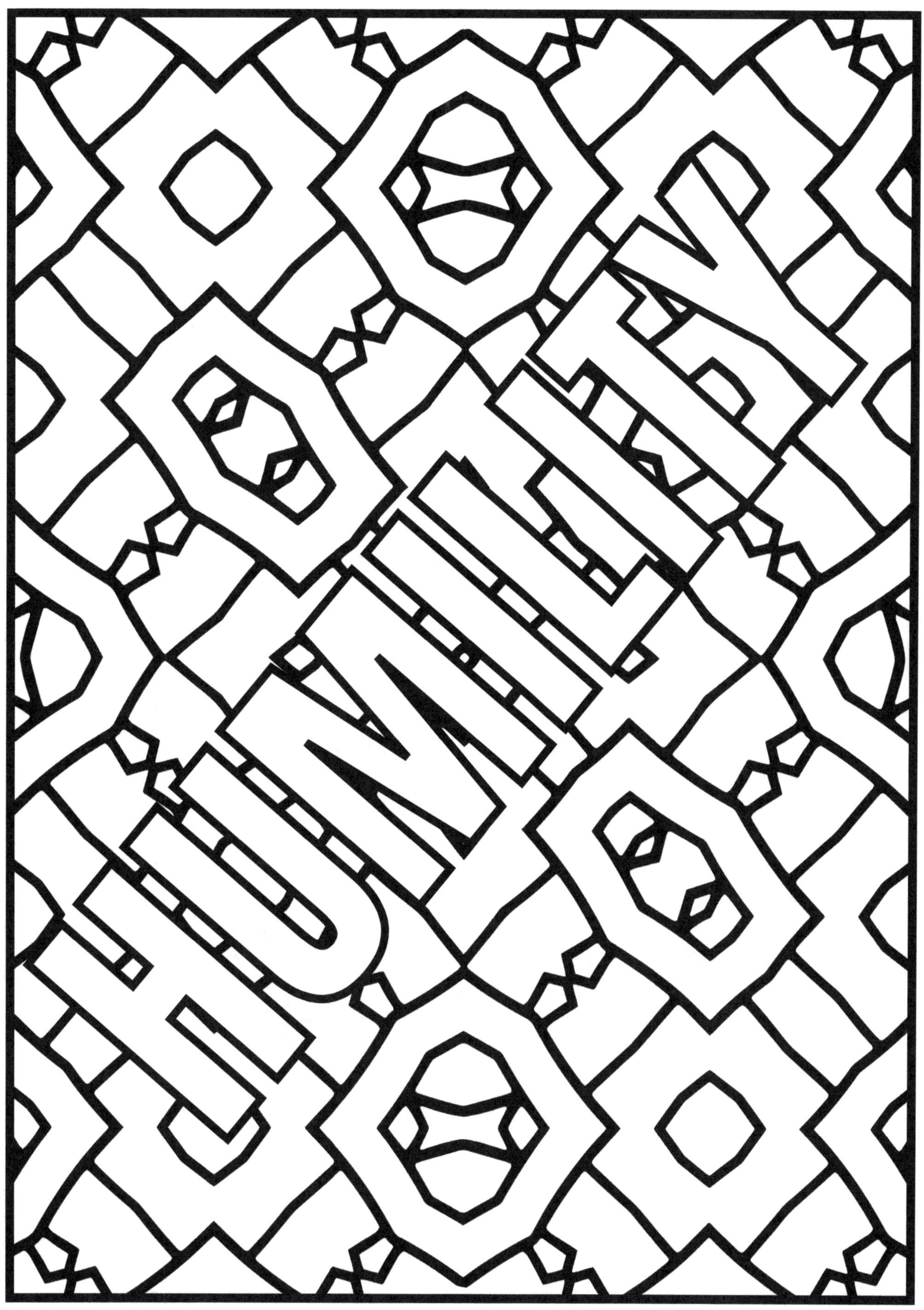
HUMILITY

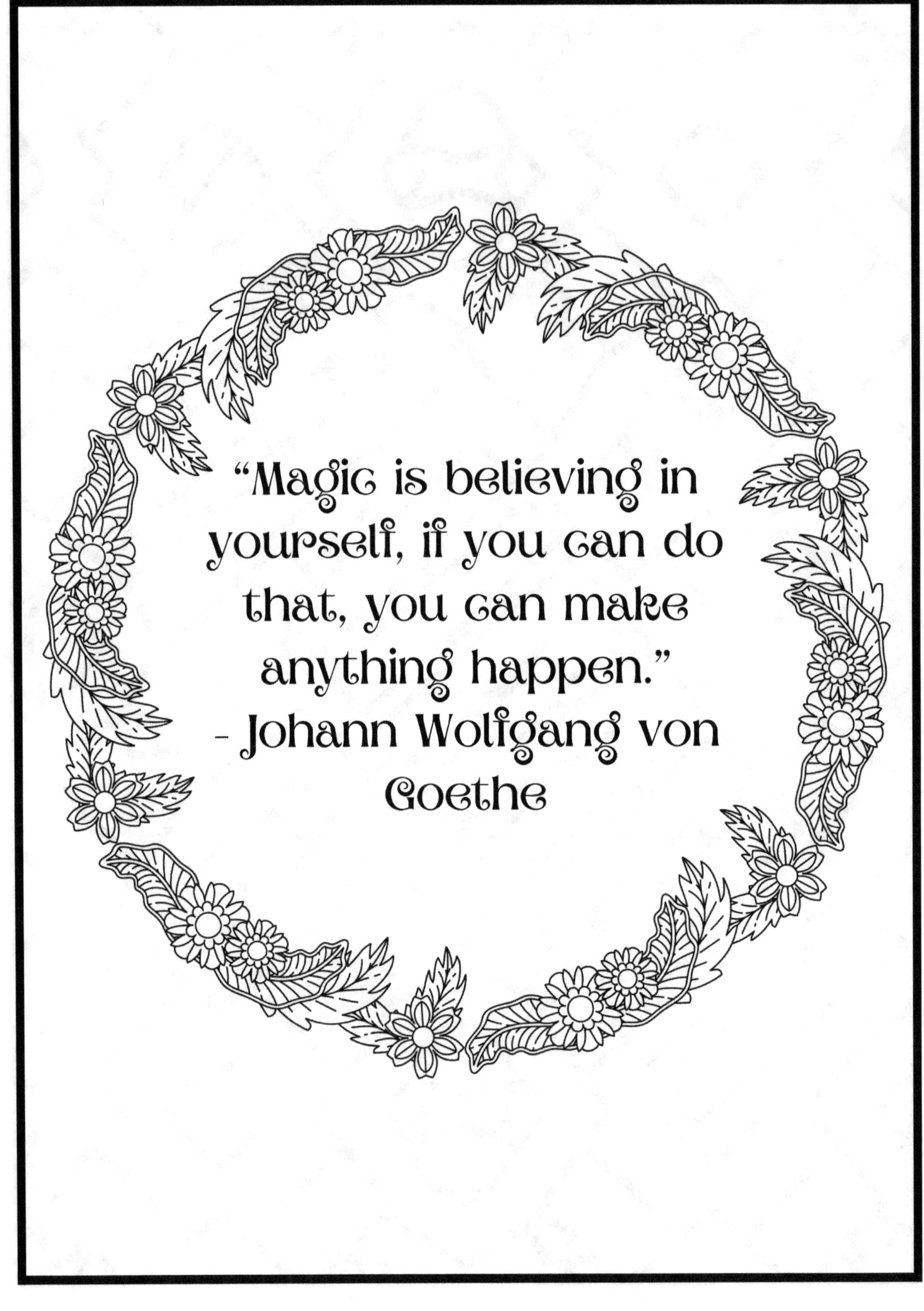
"Magic is believing in
yourself, if you can do
that, you can make
anything happen."
- Johann Wolfgang von
Goethe

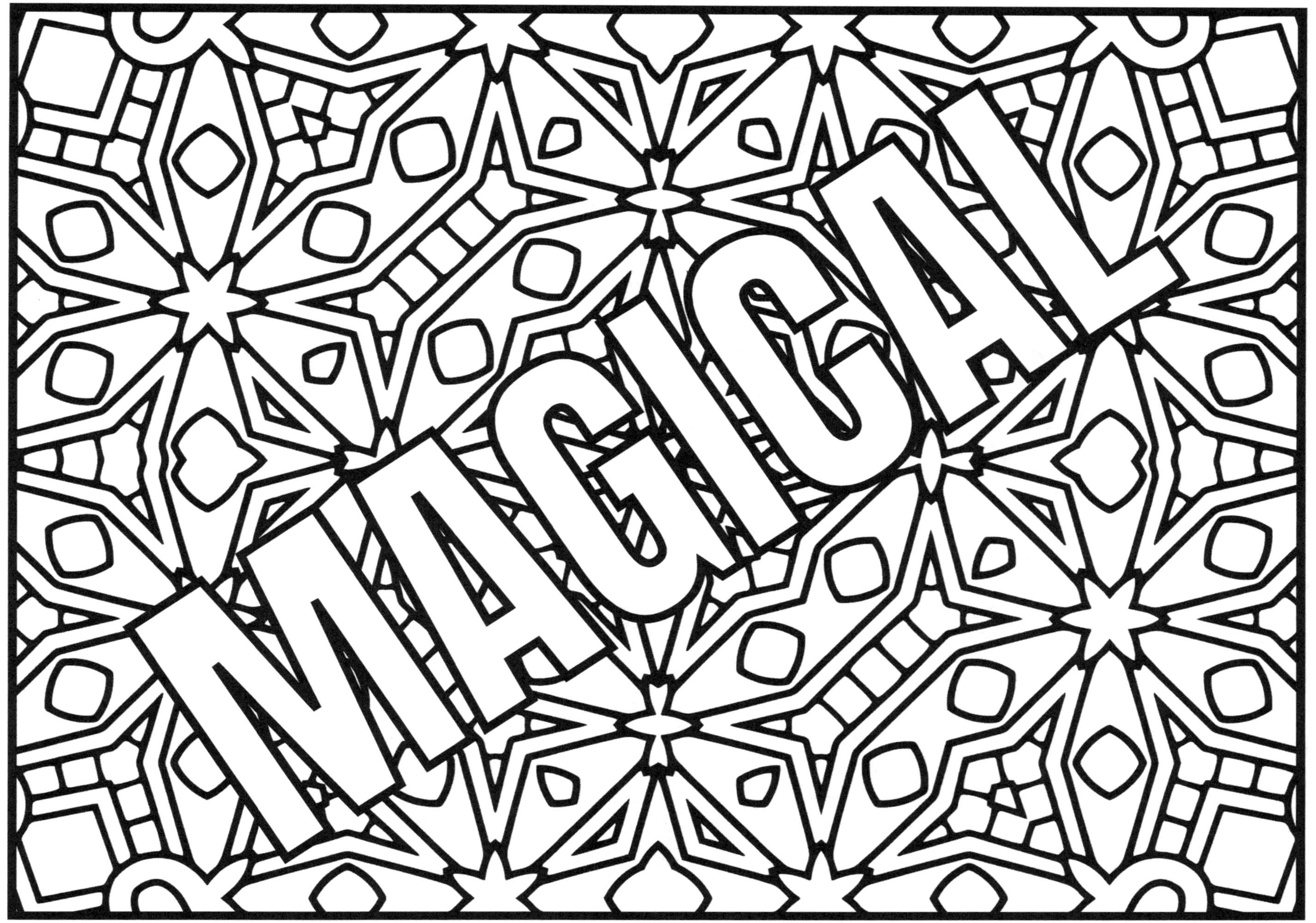
MAGICAL

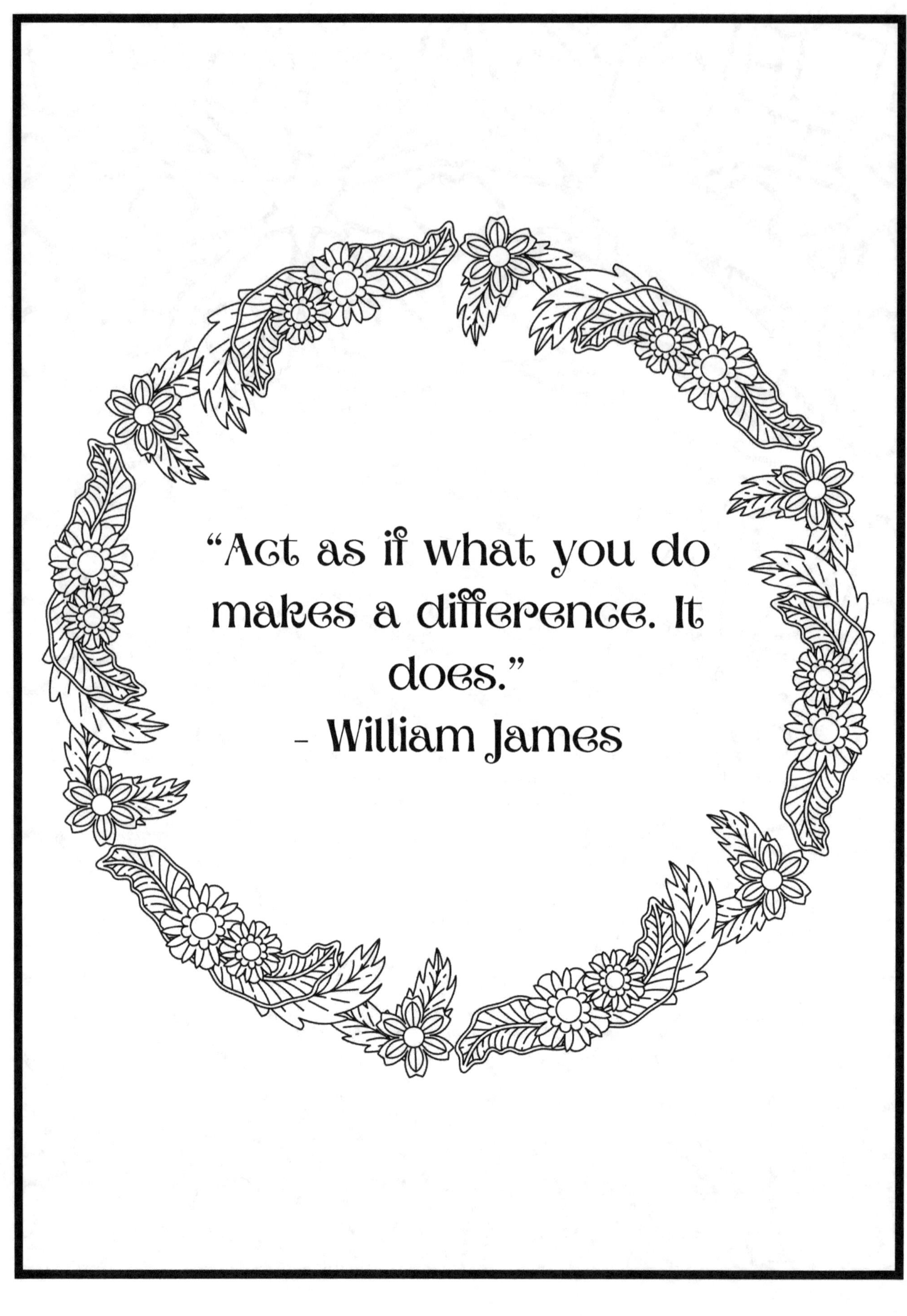
"Act as if what you do
makes a difference. It
does."
- William James

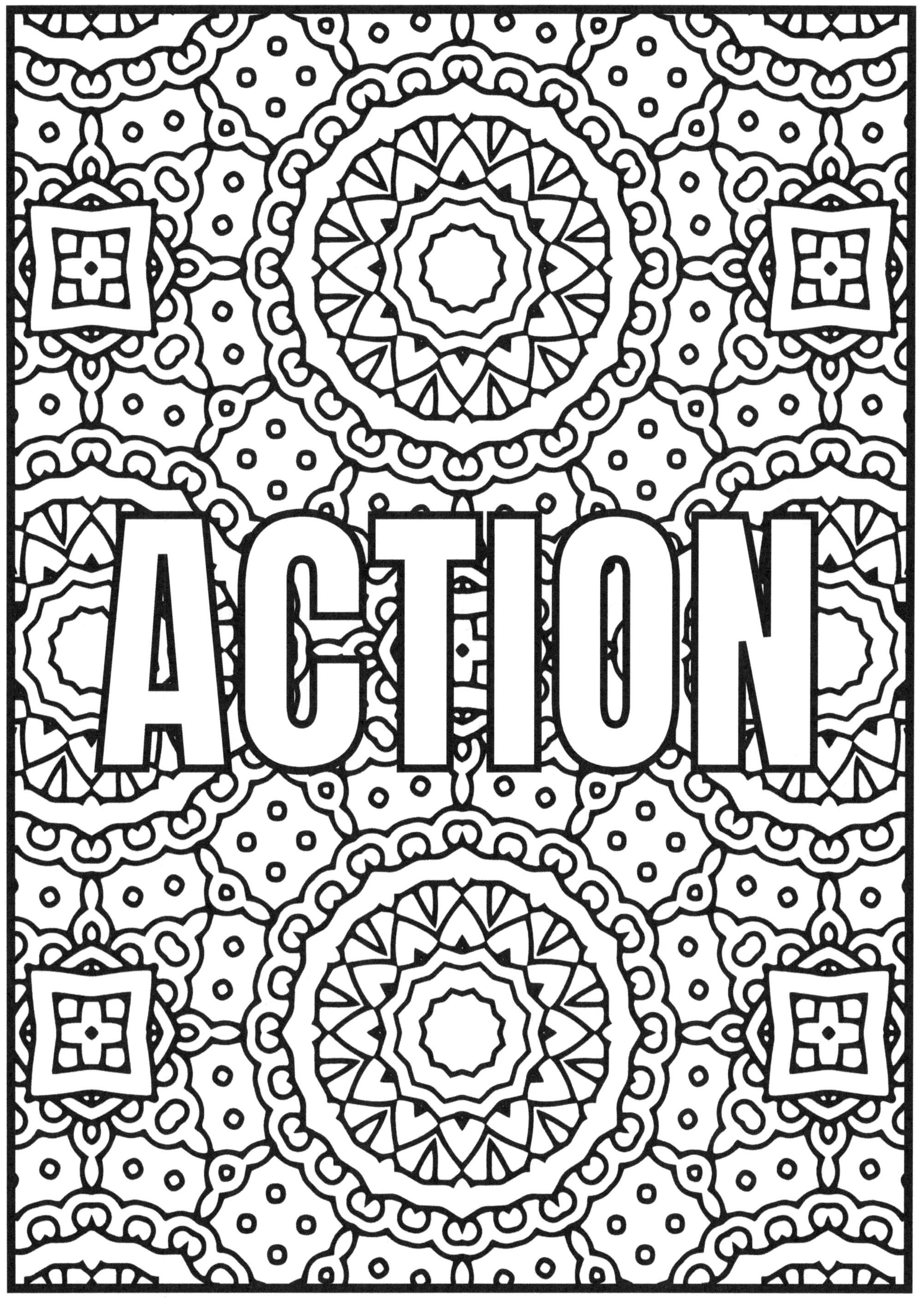
ACTION

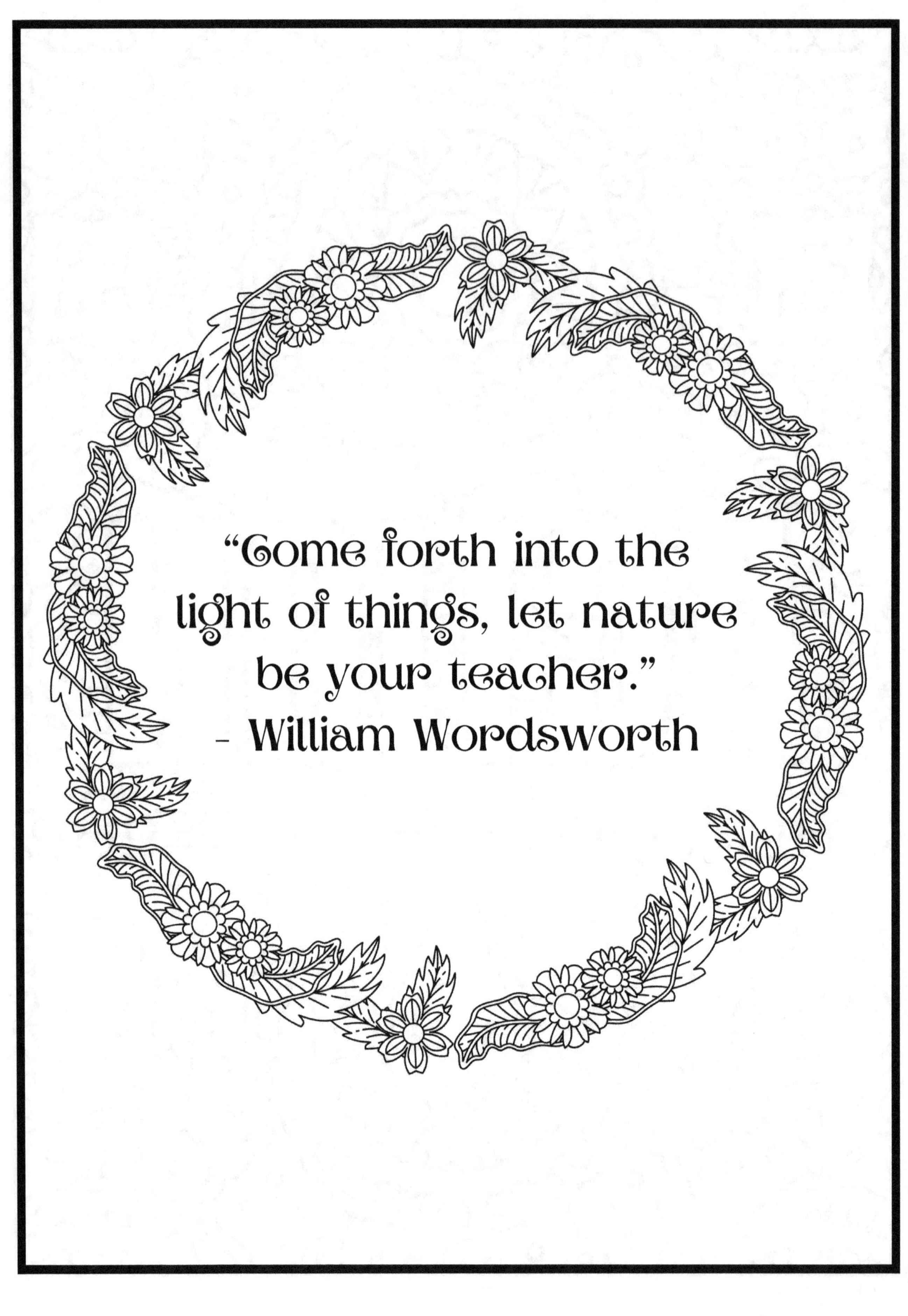
"Come forth into the
light of things, let nature
be your teacher."
- William Wordsworth

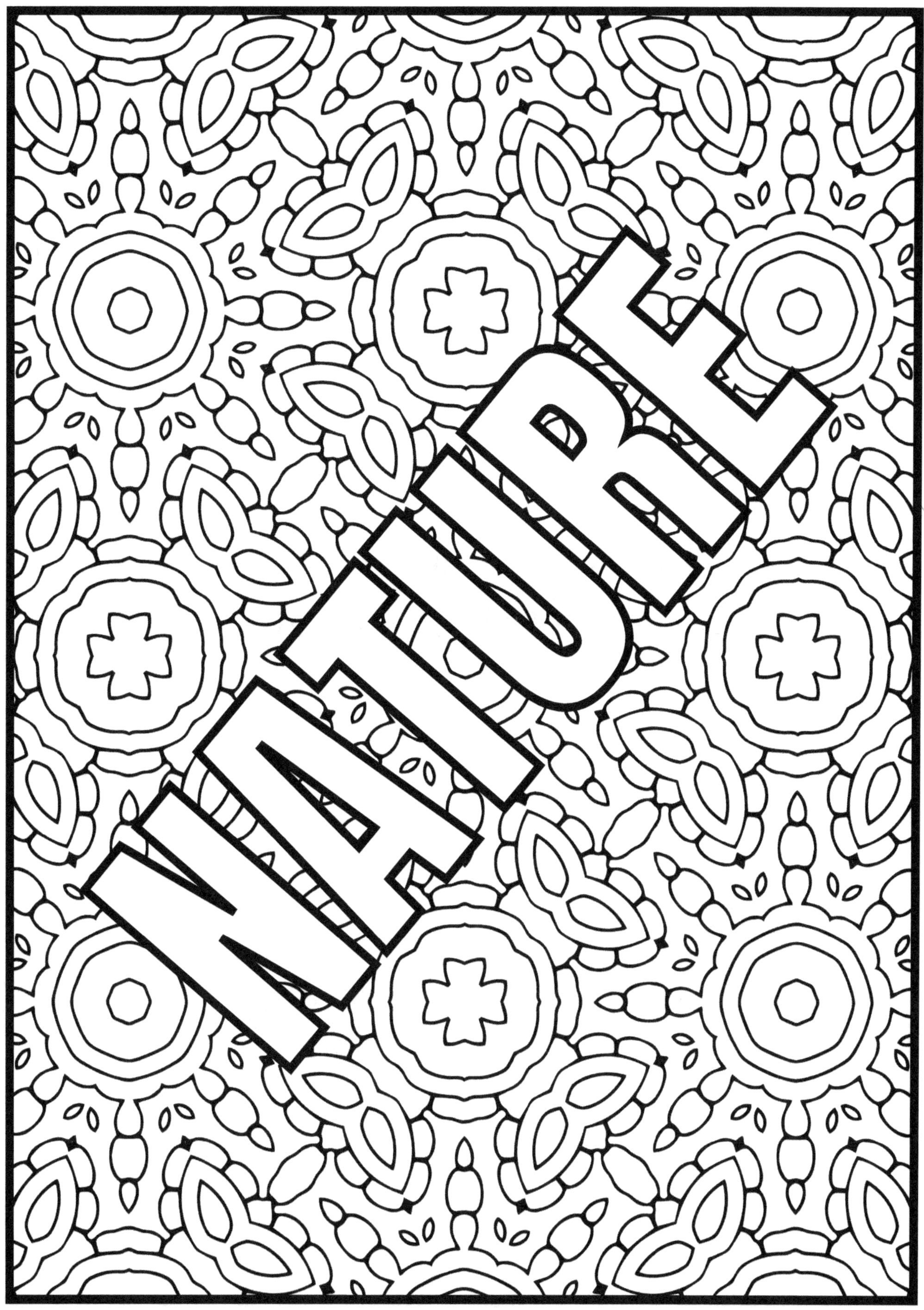
NATURE

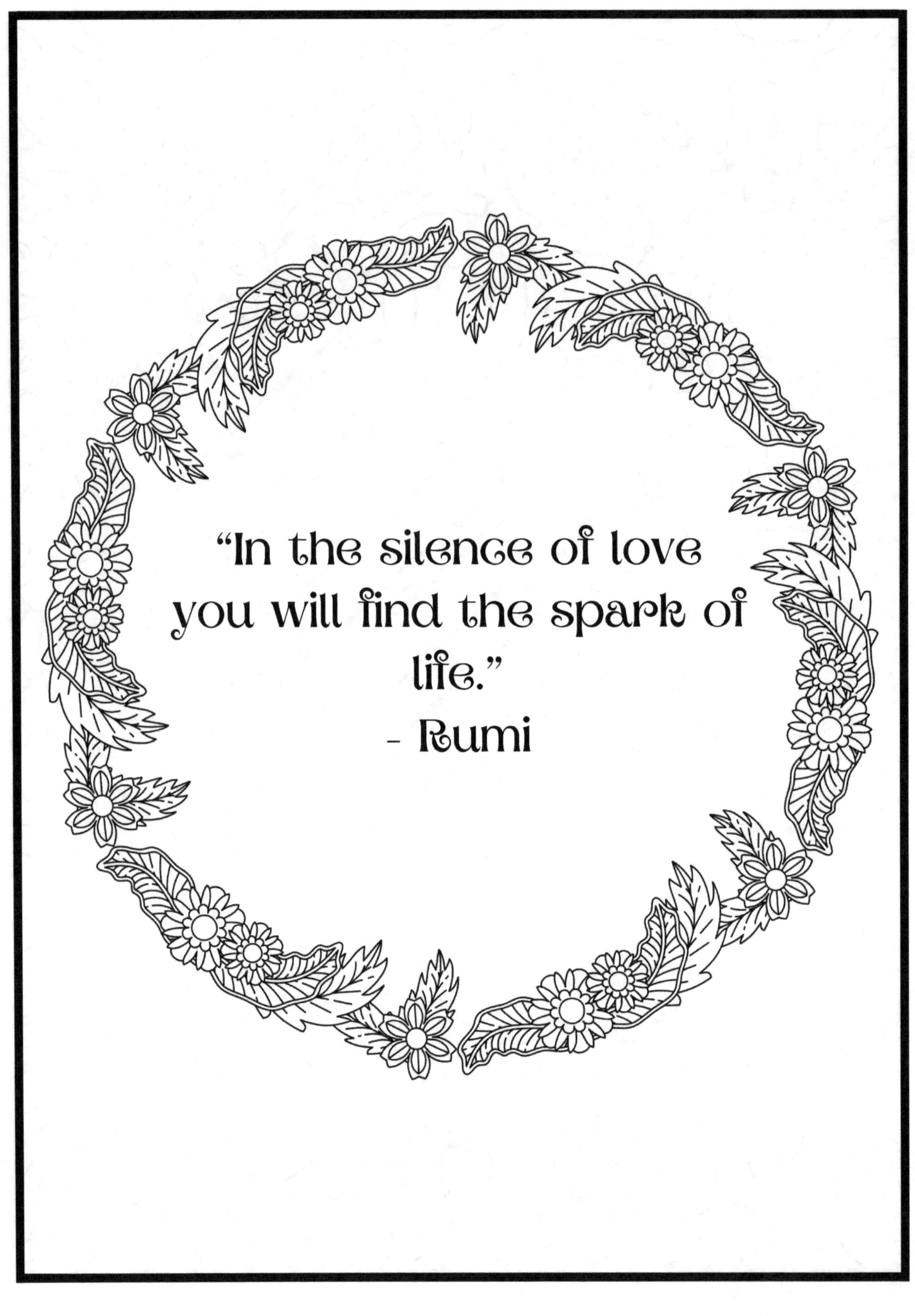
"In the silence of love
you will find the spark of
life."
- Rumi

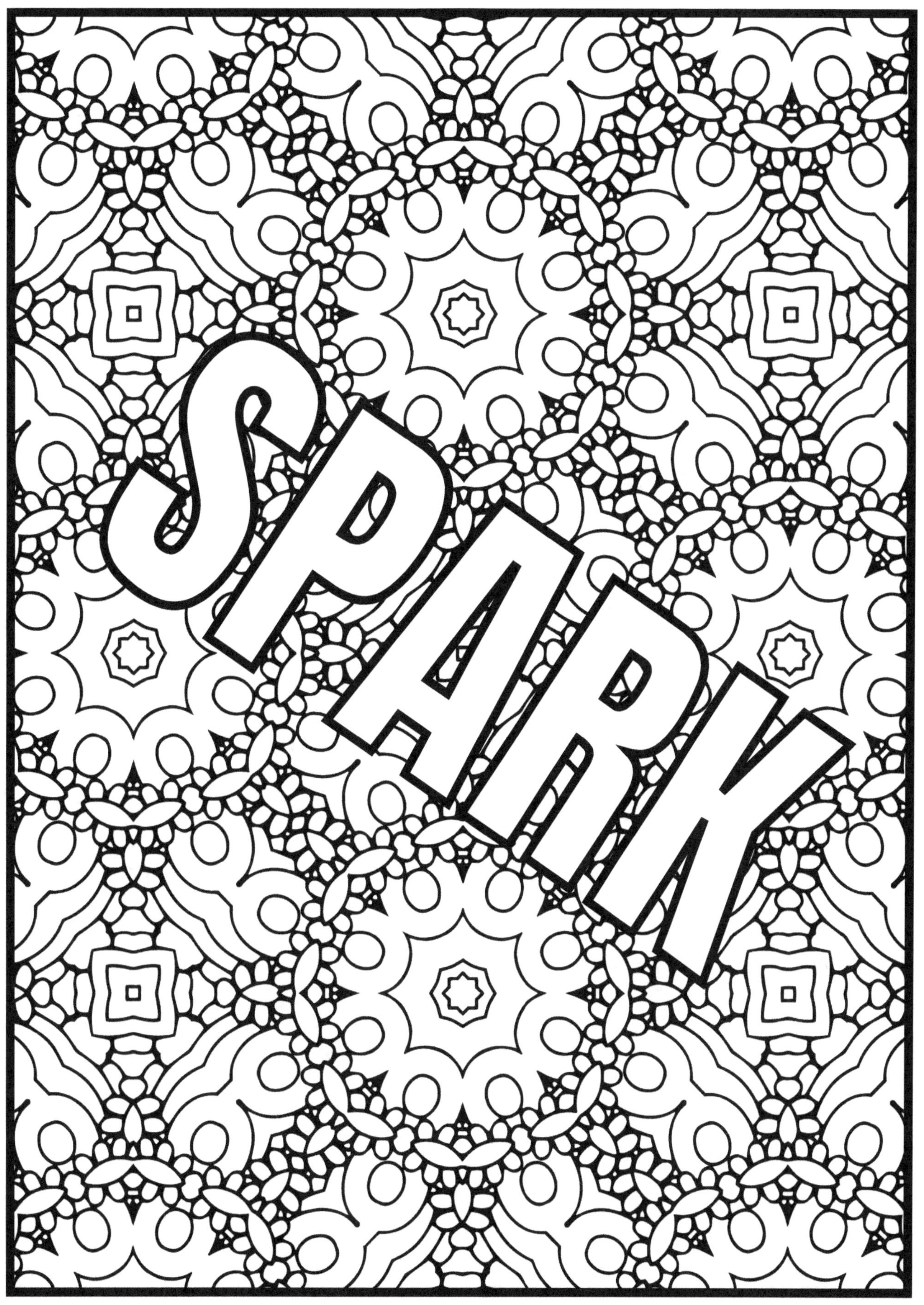
SPARK

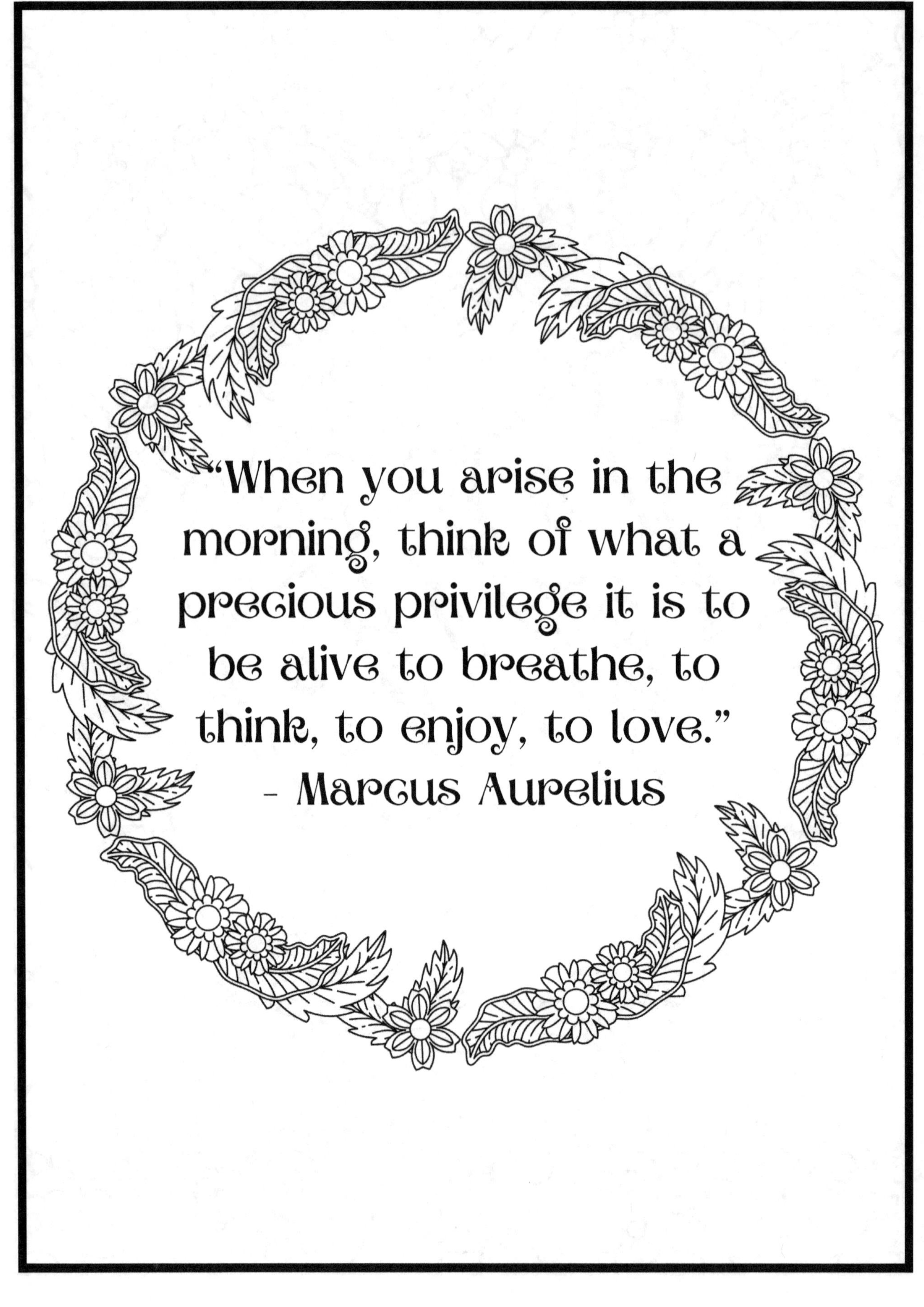
"When you arise in the
morning, think of what a
precious privilege it is to
be alive to breathe, to
think, to enjoy, to love."
- Marcus Aurelius

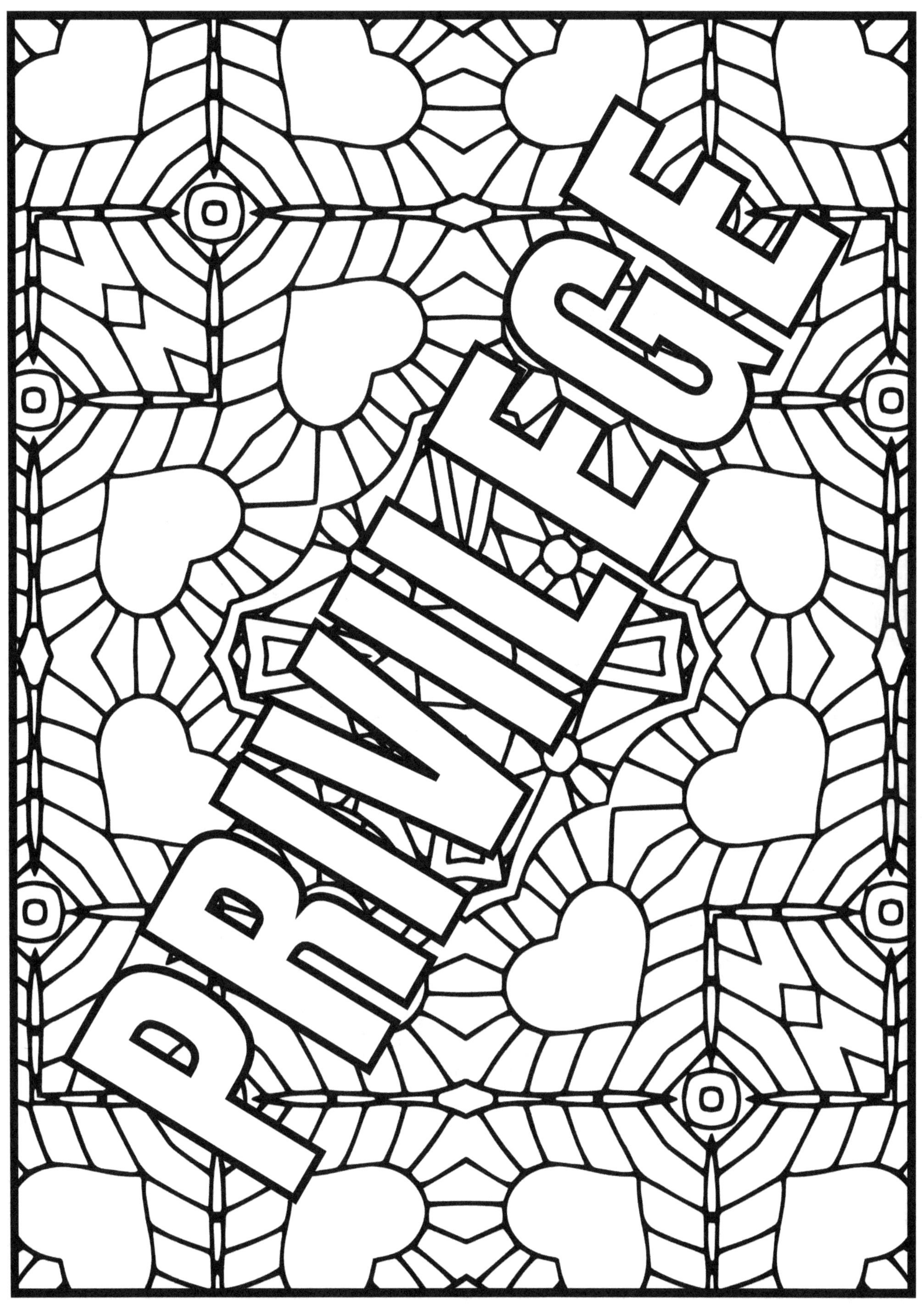
PRIVILEGE

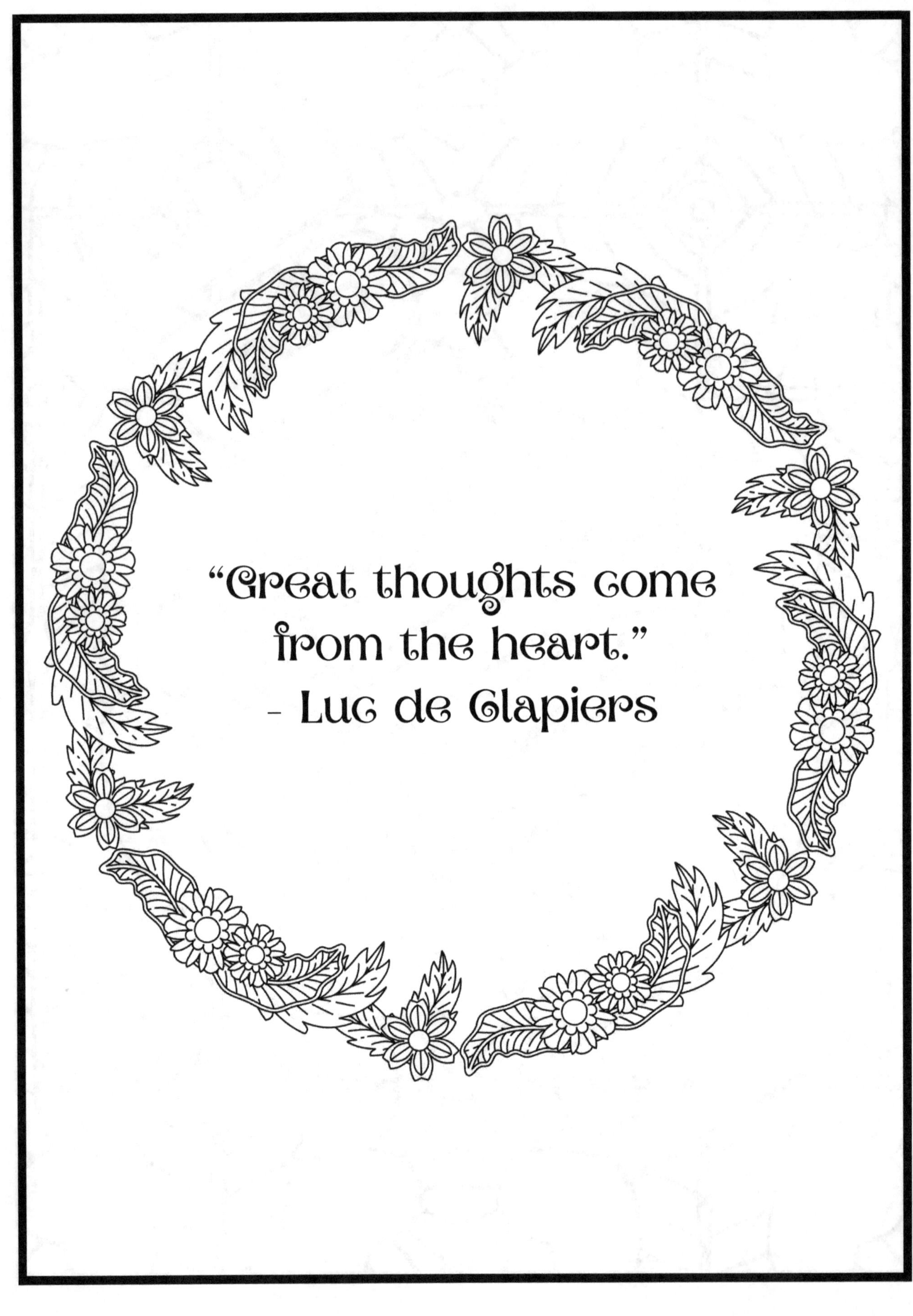
"Great thoughts come
from the heart."
- Luc de Clapiers

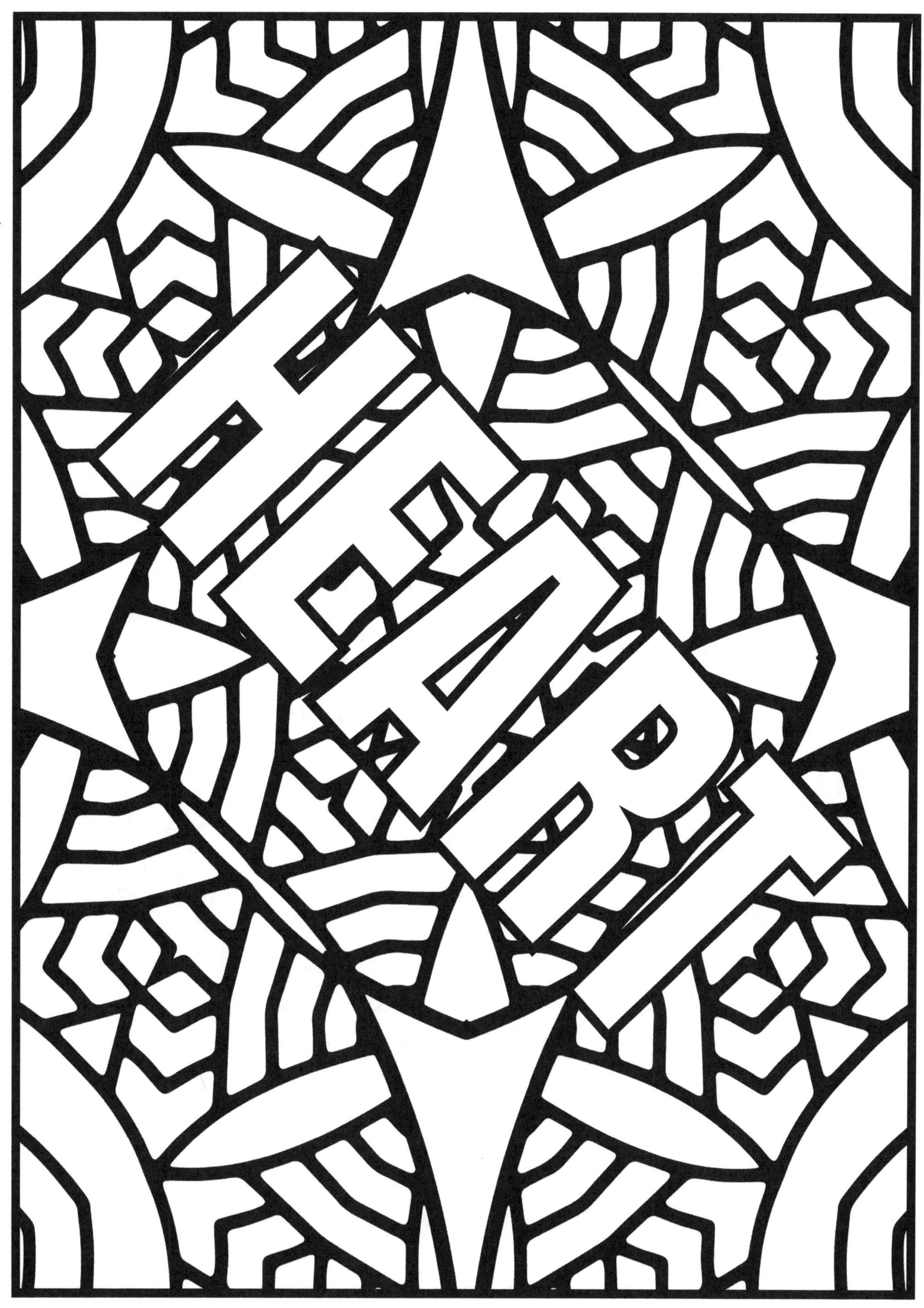
HEART

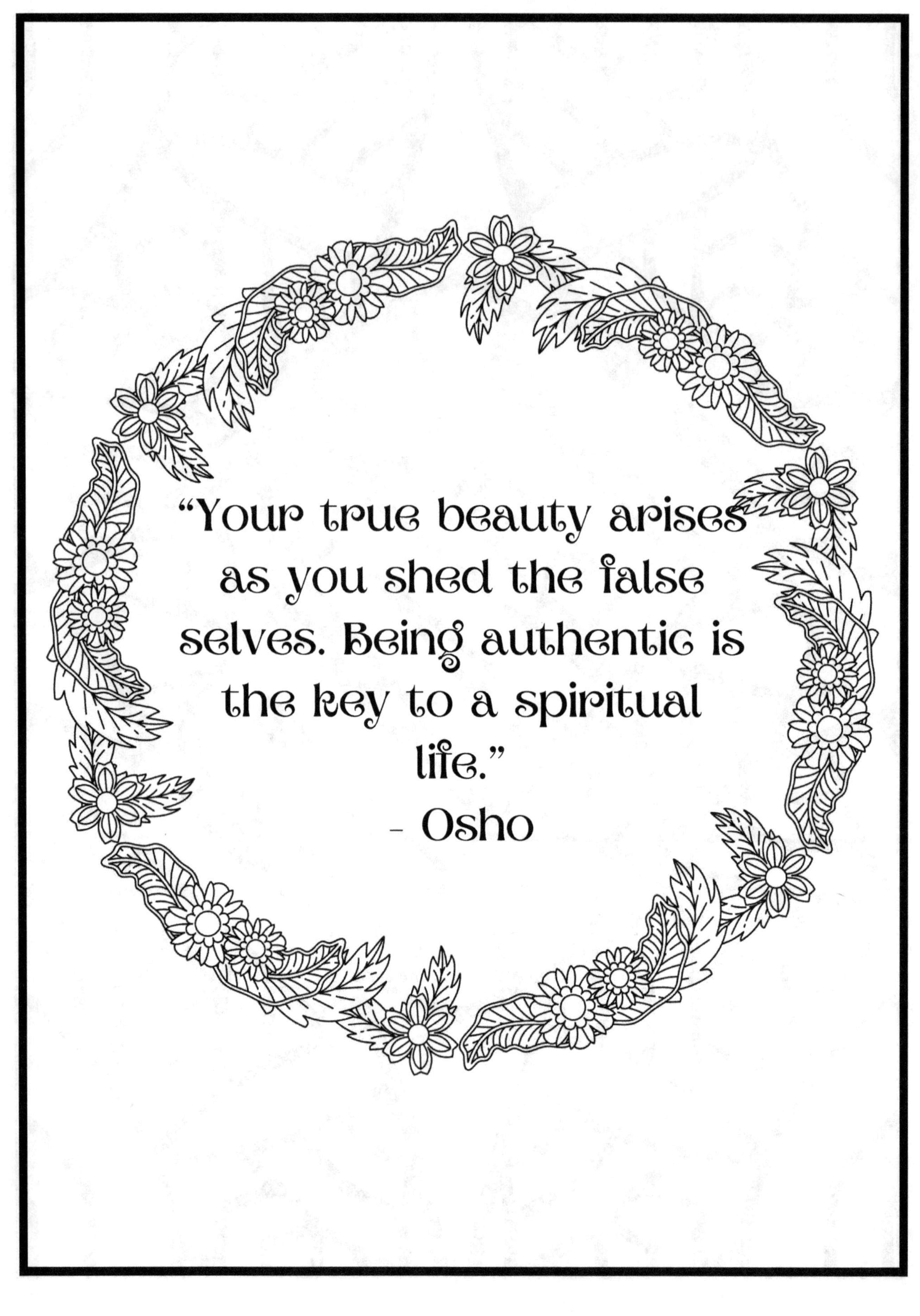
"Your true beauty arises
as you shed the false
selves. Being authentic is
the key to a spiritual
life."
- Osho

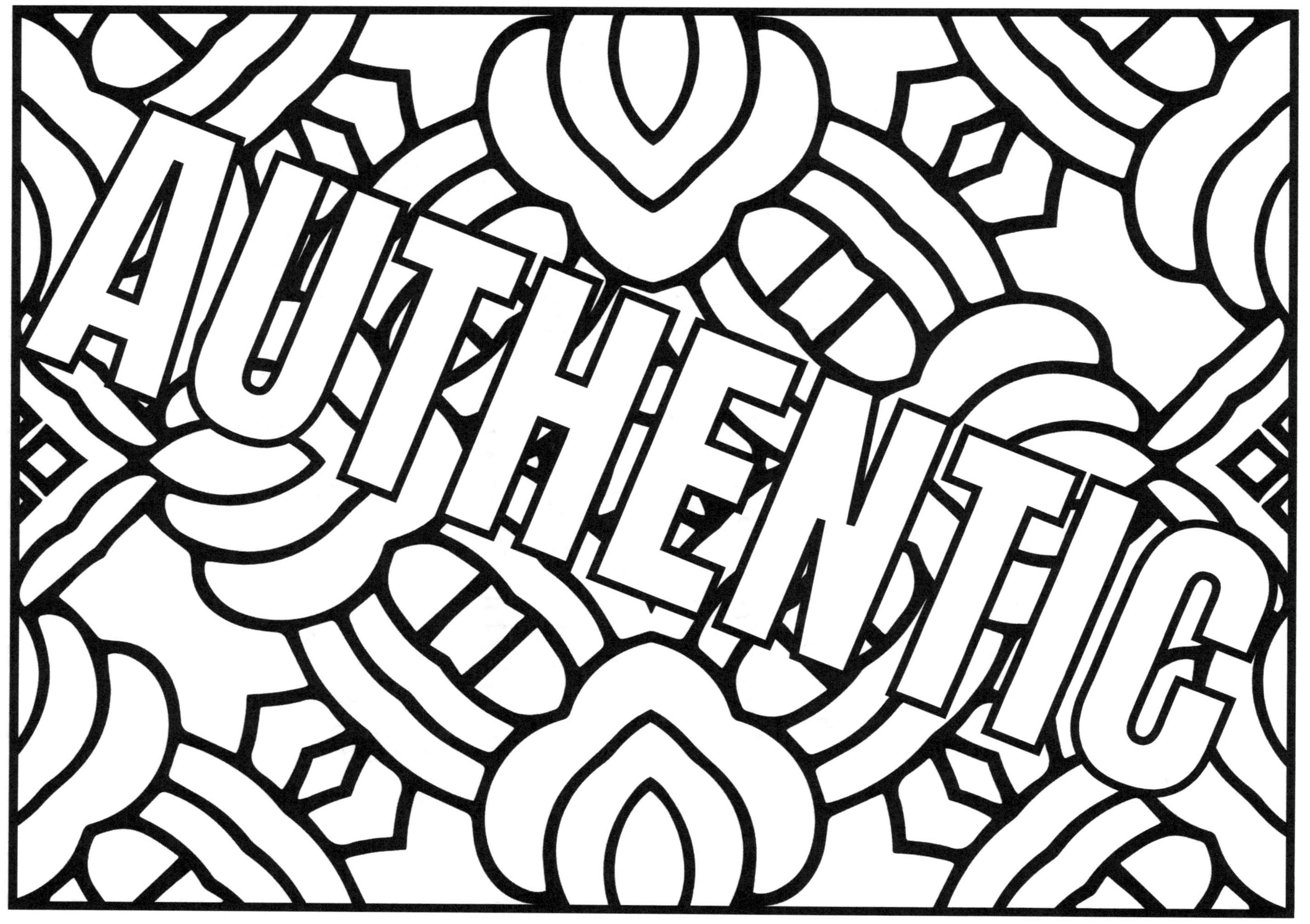
AUTHENTIC

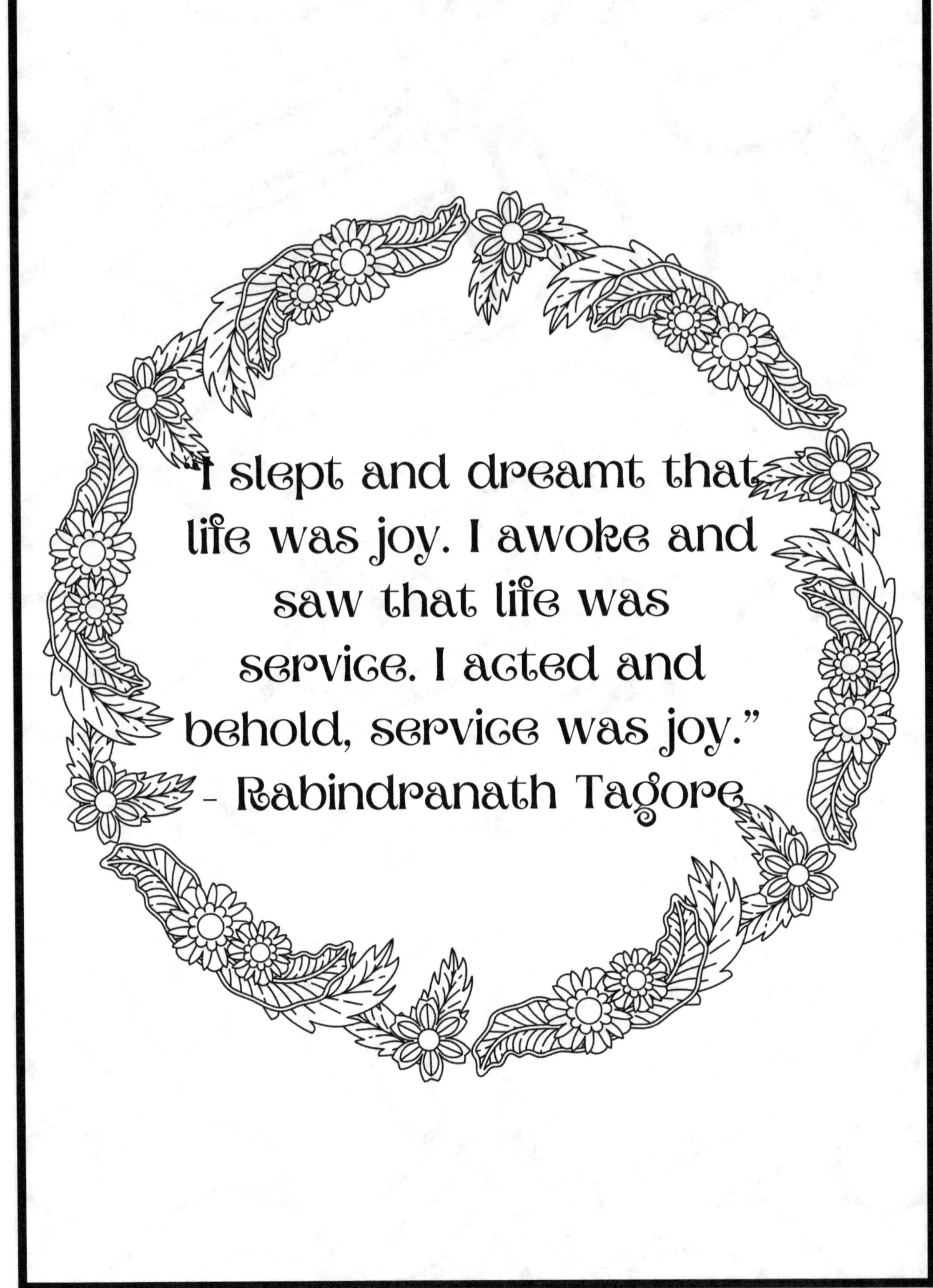
"I slept and dreamt that
life was joy. I awoke and
saw that life was
service. I acted and
behold, service was joy."
- Rabindranath Tagore

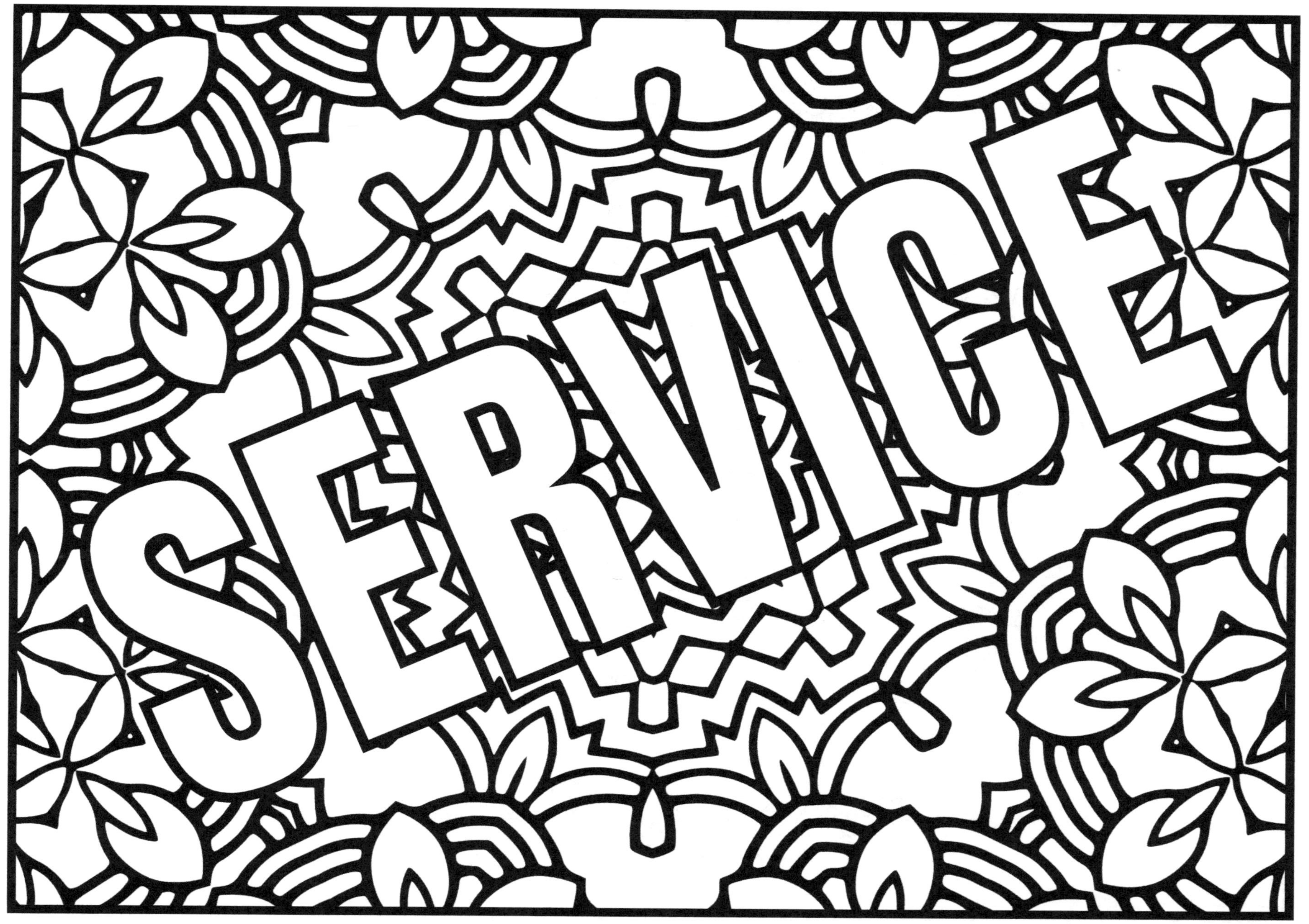
SERVICE

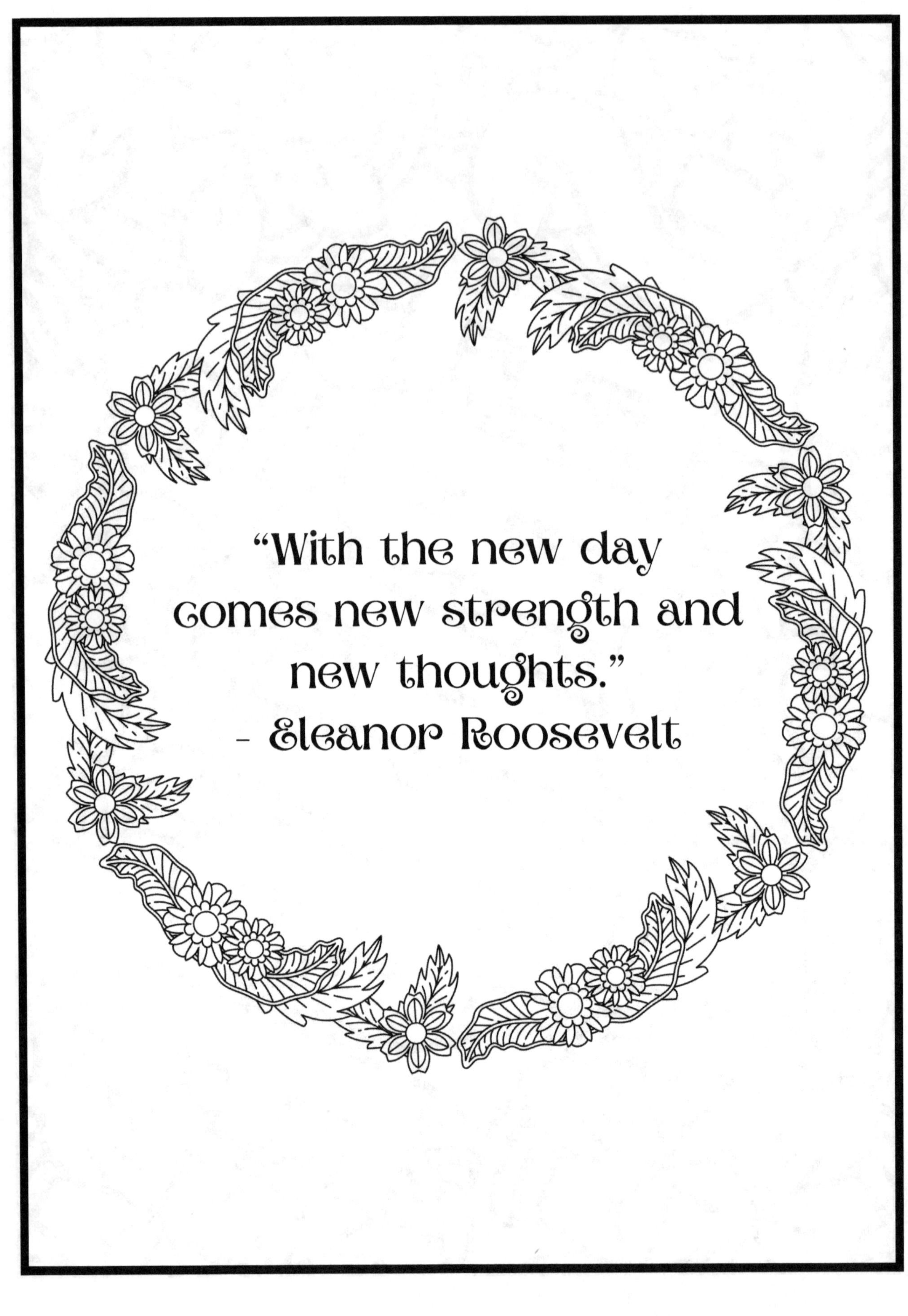
"With the new day
comes new strength and
new thoughts."
- Eleanor Roosevelt

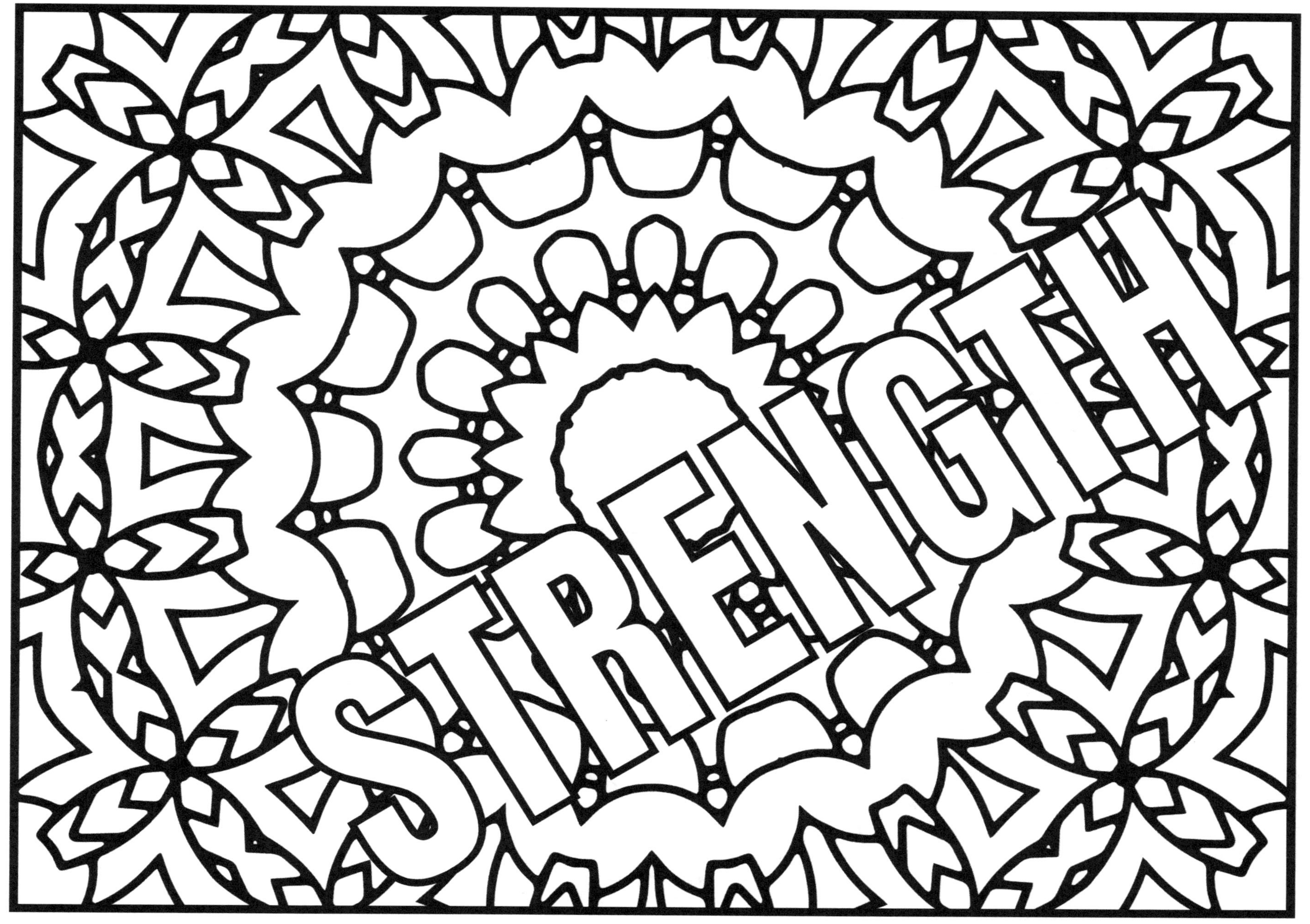
STRENGTH

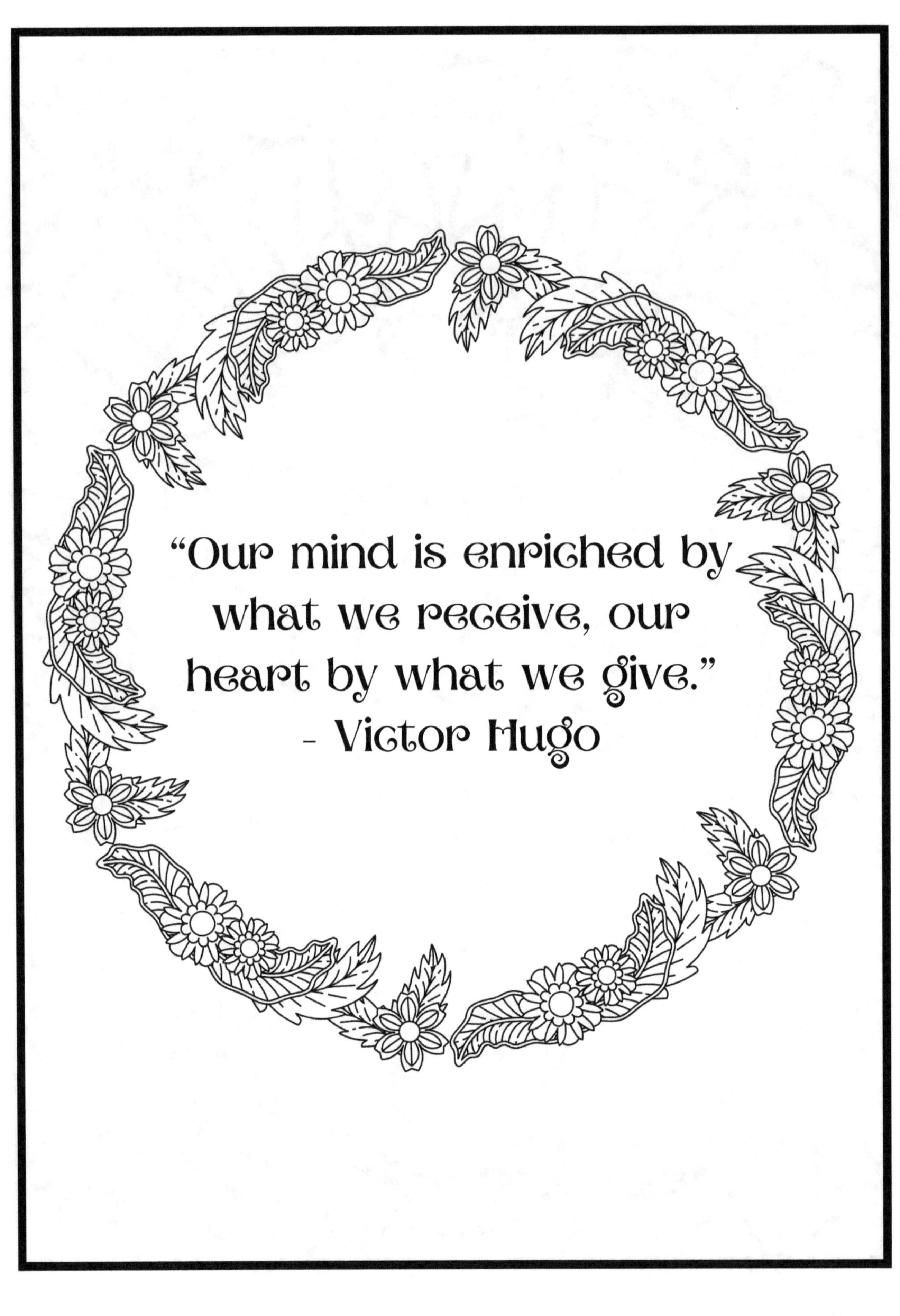
"Our mind is enriched by
what we receive, our
heart by what we give."
- Victor Hugo

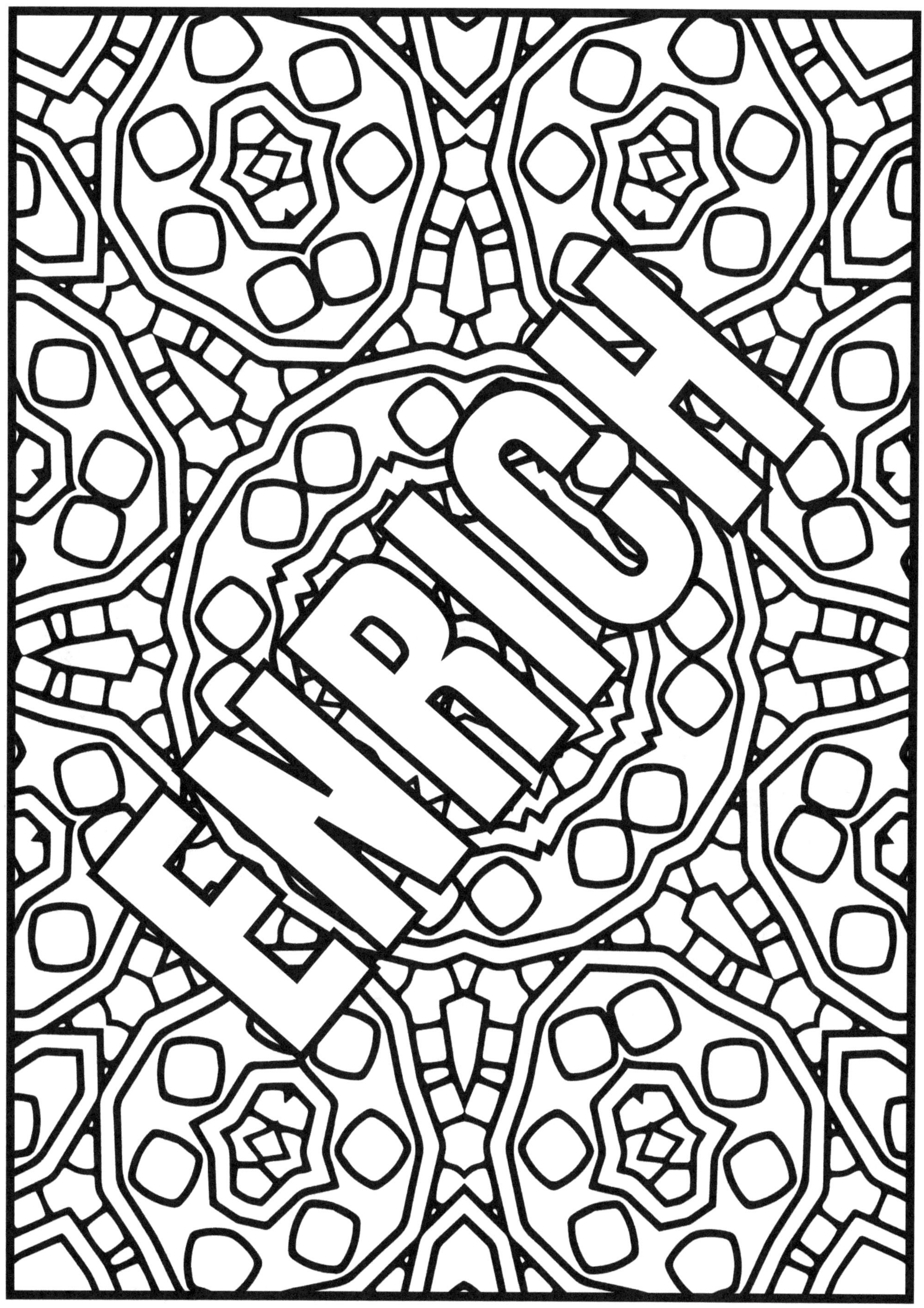
ENRICH

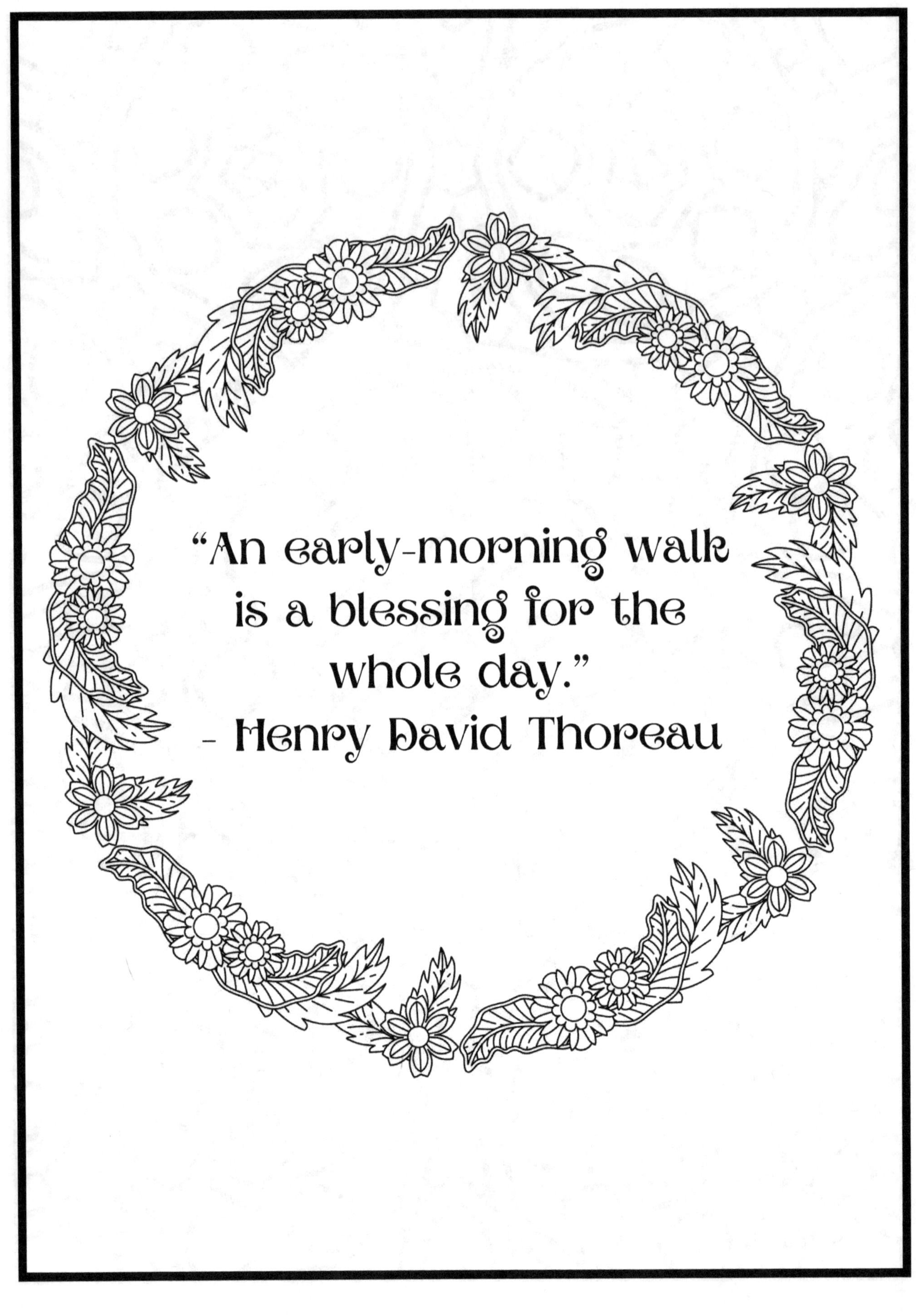
"An early-morning walk
is a blessing for the
whole day."
- Henry David Thoreau

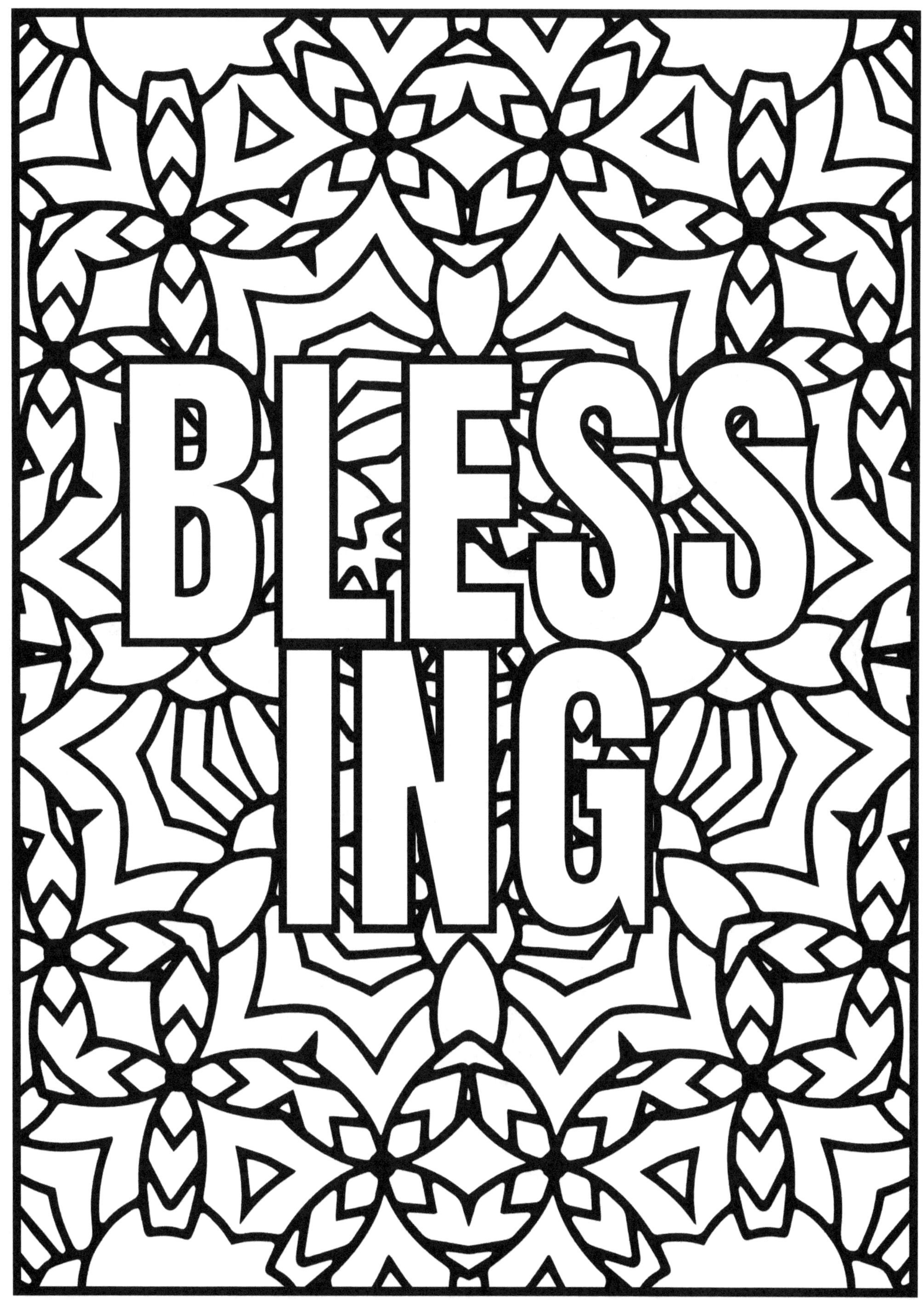
BLESS
ING

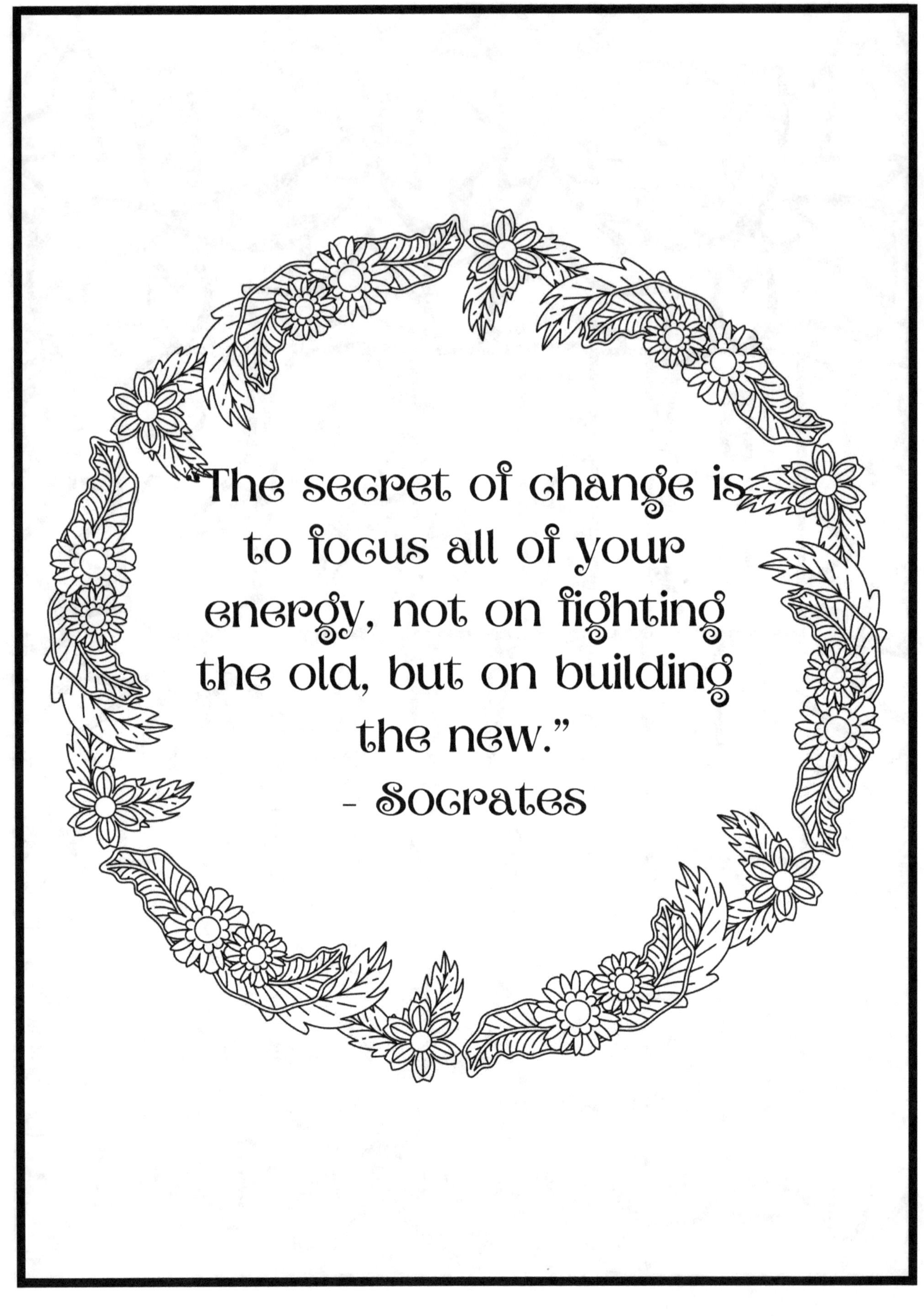
"The secret of change is
to focus all of your
energy, not on fighting
the old, but on building
the new."
- Socrates

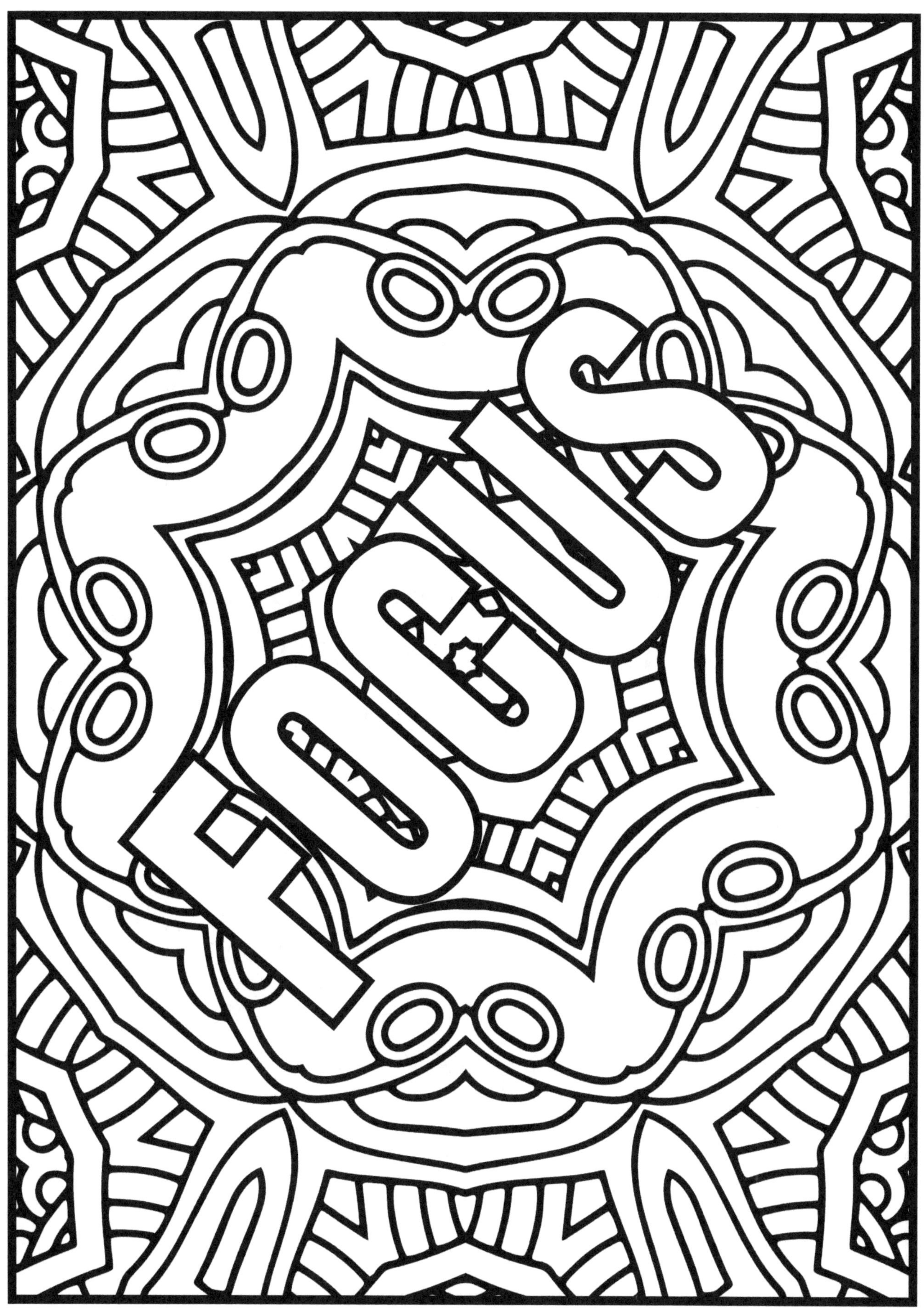
FOCUS

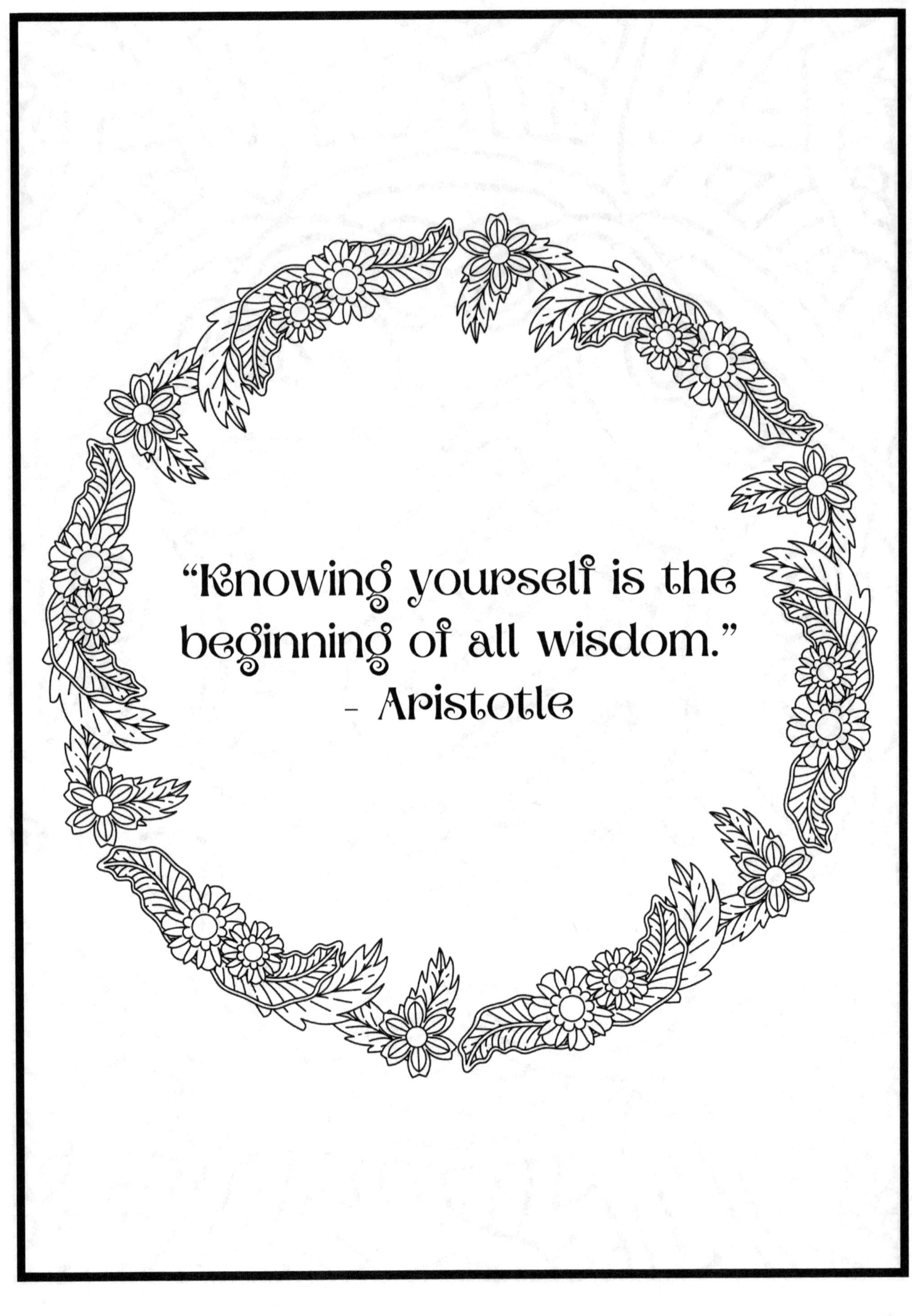
"Knowing yourself is the
beginning of all wisdom."
- Aristotle

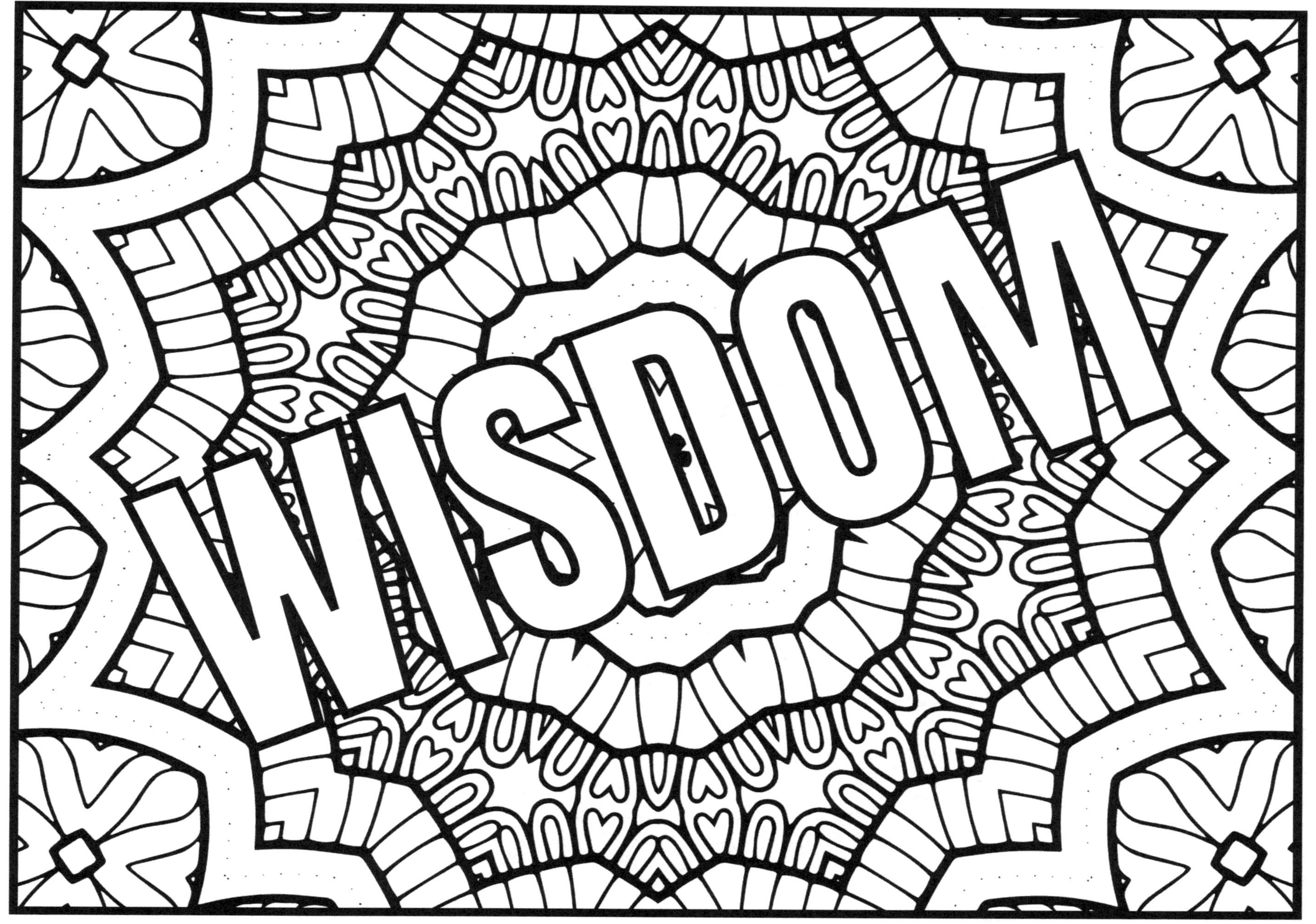
WISDOM

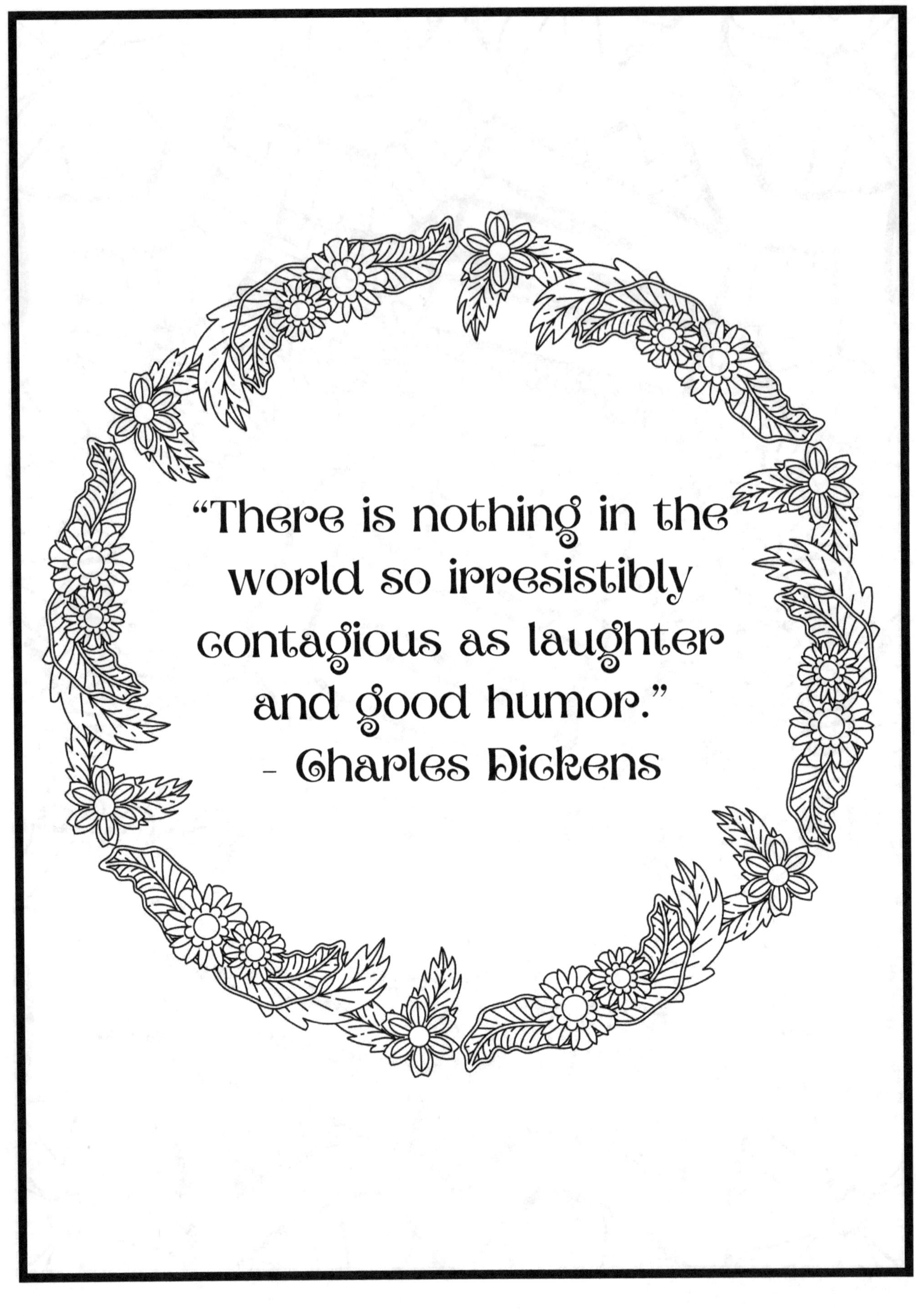
"There is nothing in the world so irresistibly contagious as laughter and good humor."
- Charles Dickens

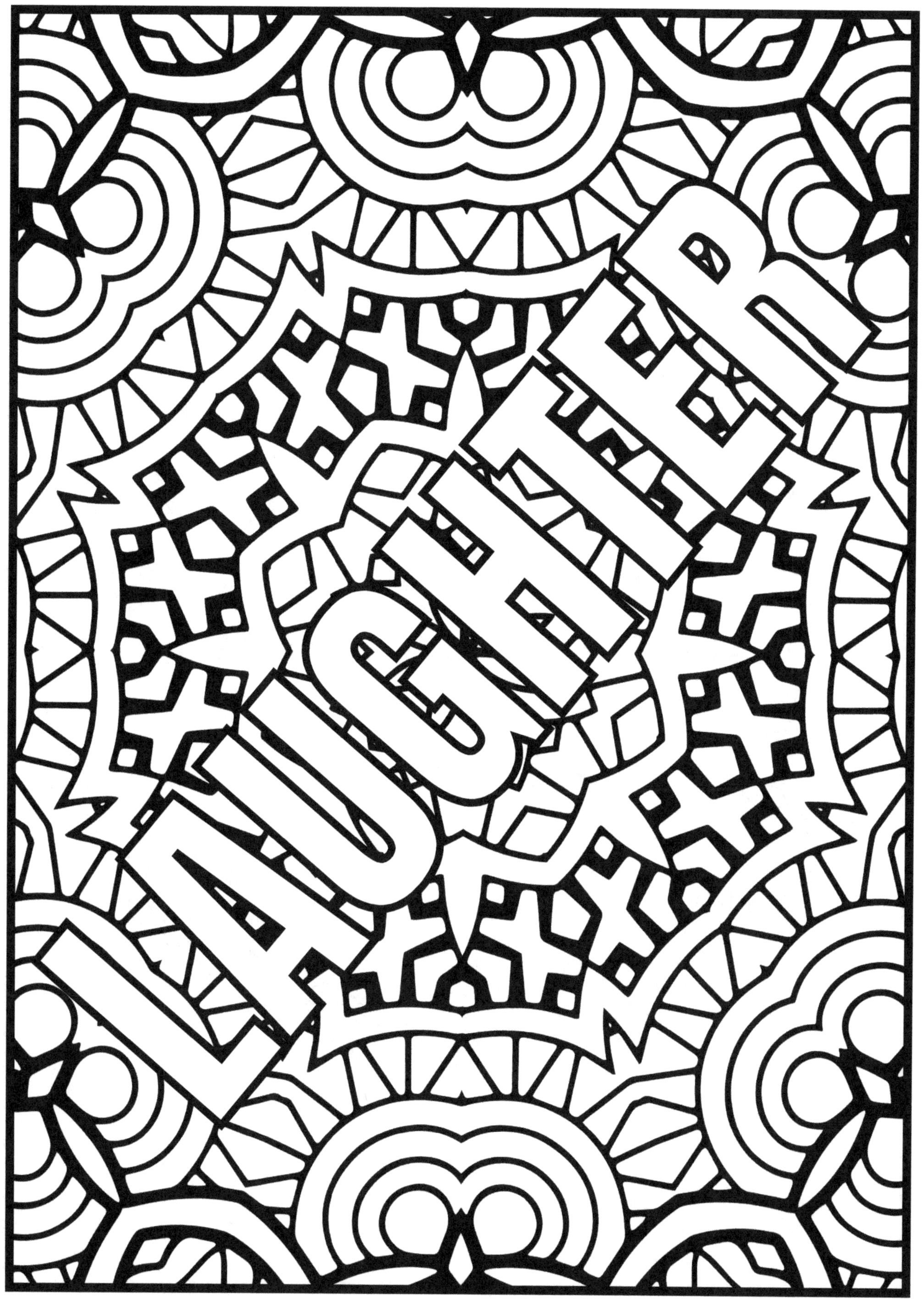
LAUGHTER

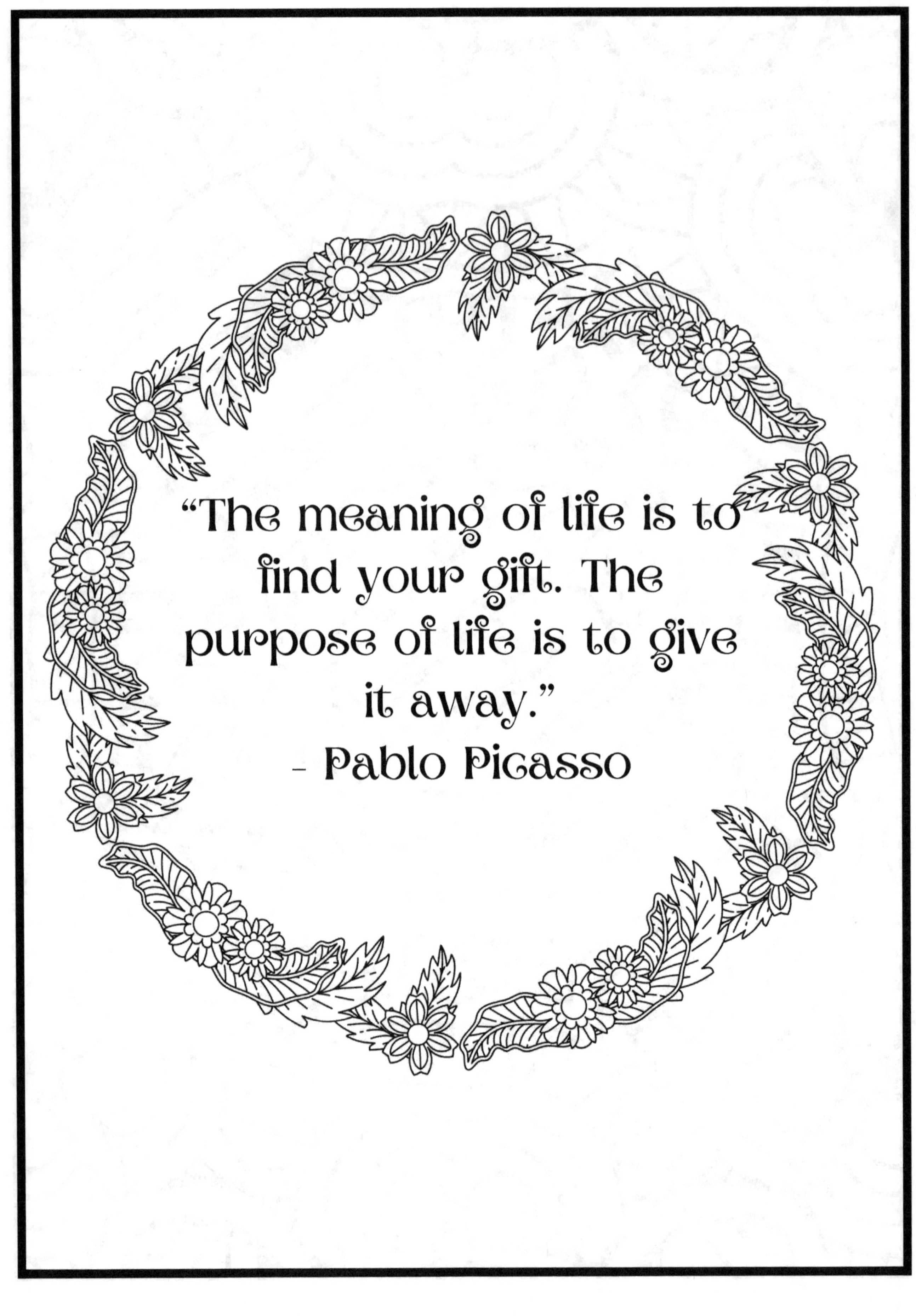
"The meaning of life is to
find your gift. The
purpose of life is to give
it away."
- Pablo Picasso

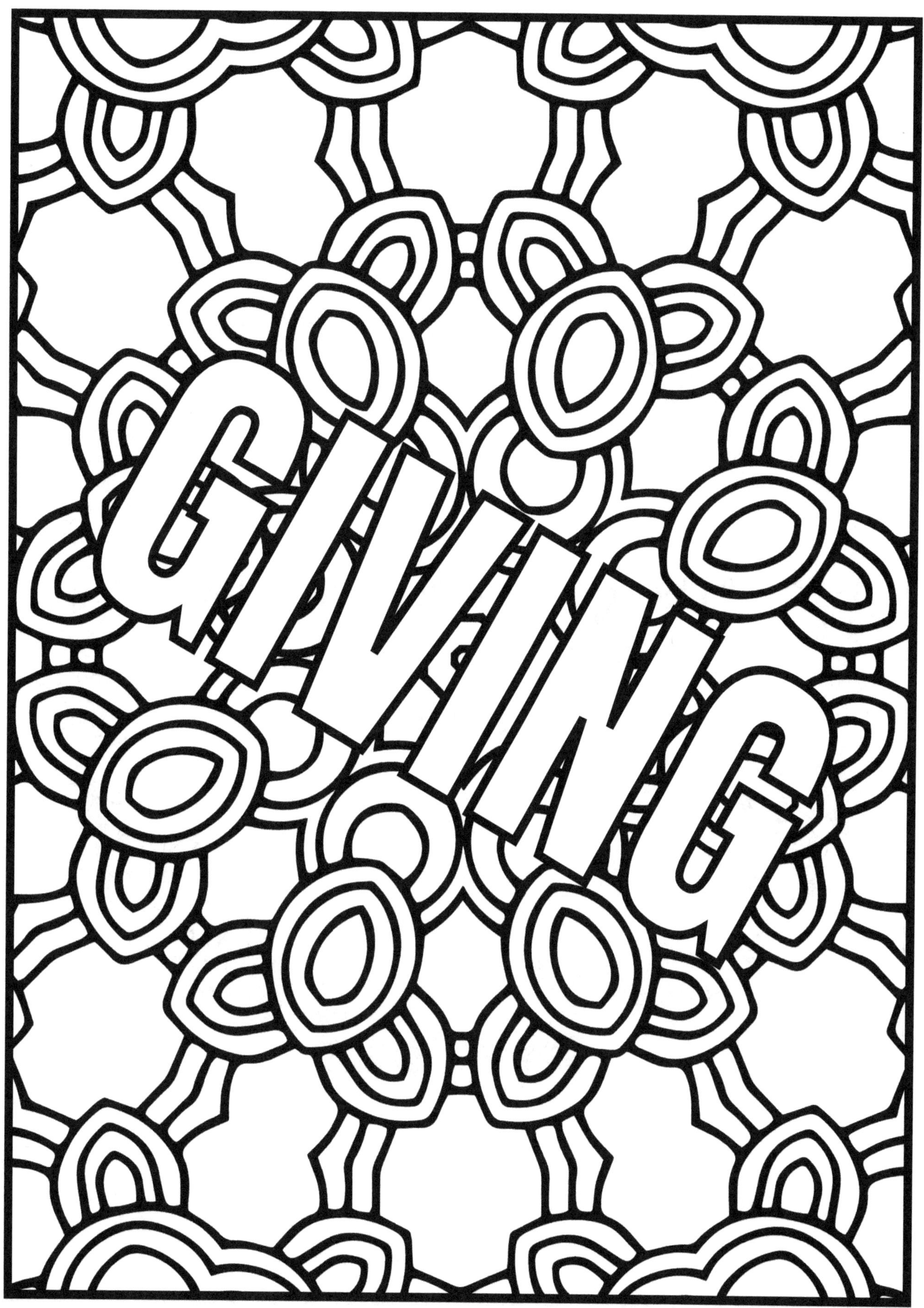
GIVING

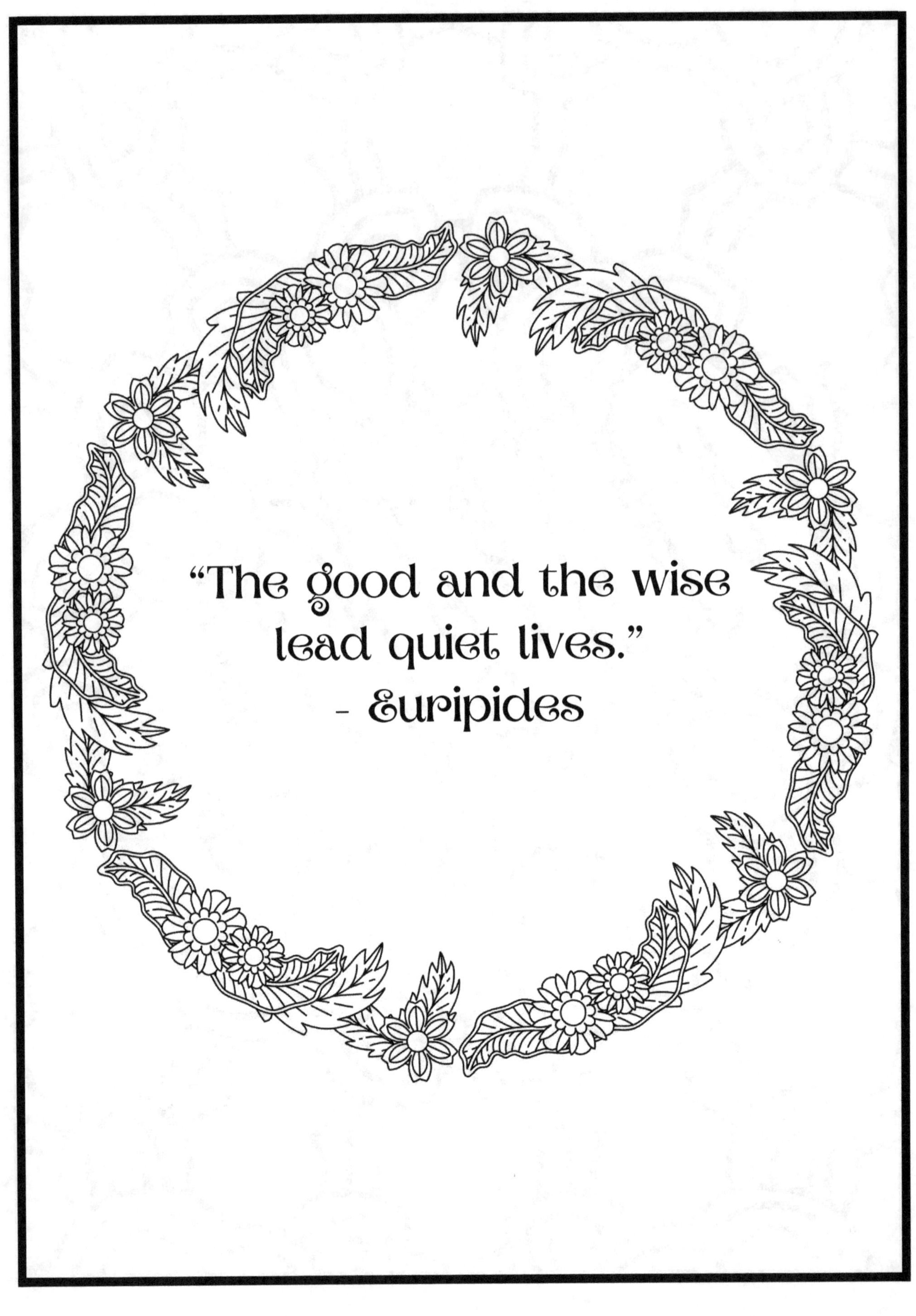
"The good and the wise
lead quiet lives."
- Euripides

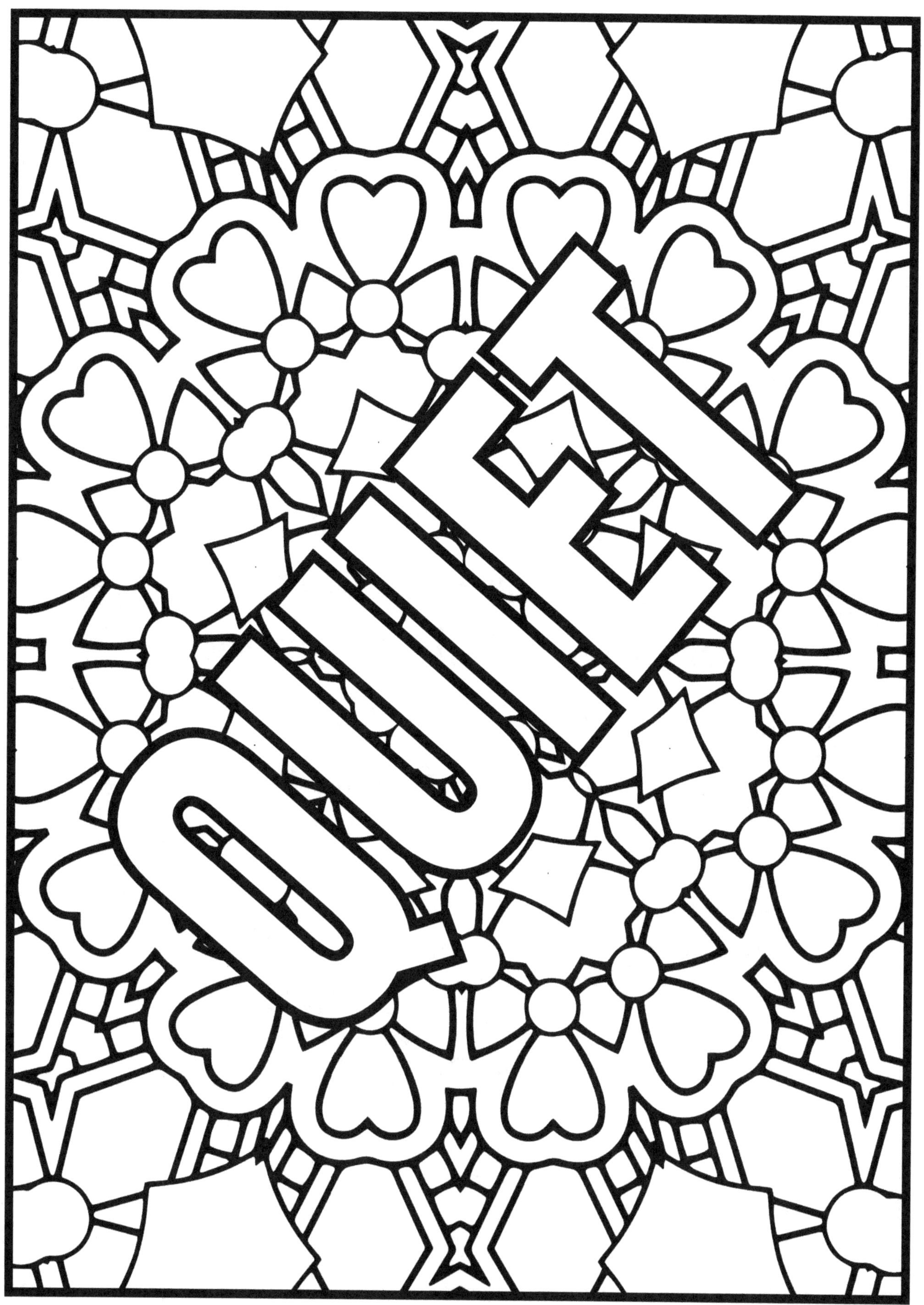
QUIET

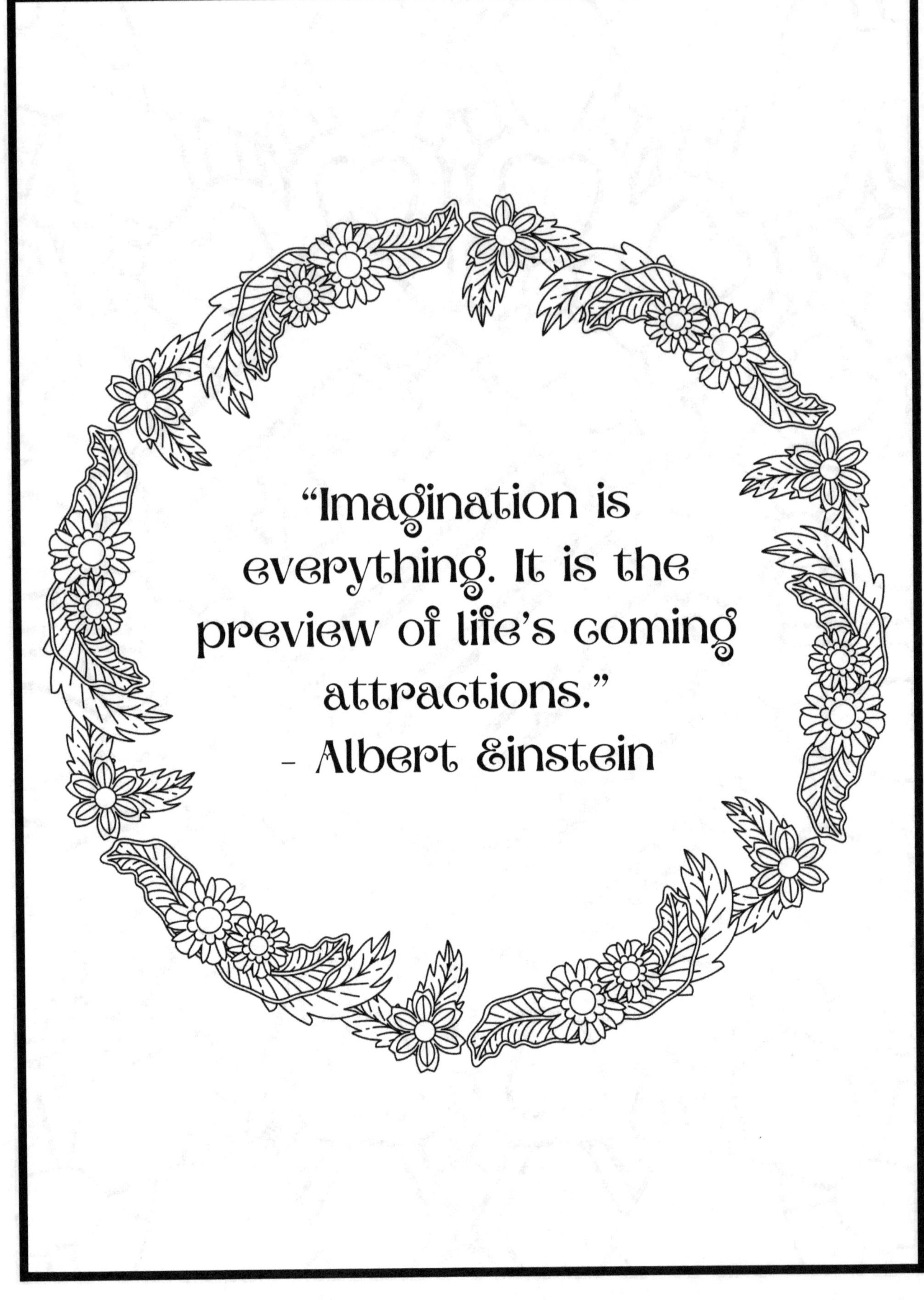
"Imagination is
everything. It is the
preview of life's coming
attractions."
- Albert Einstein

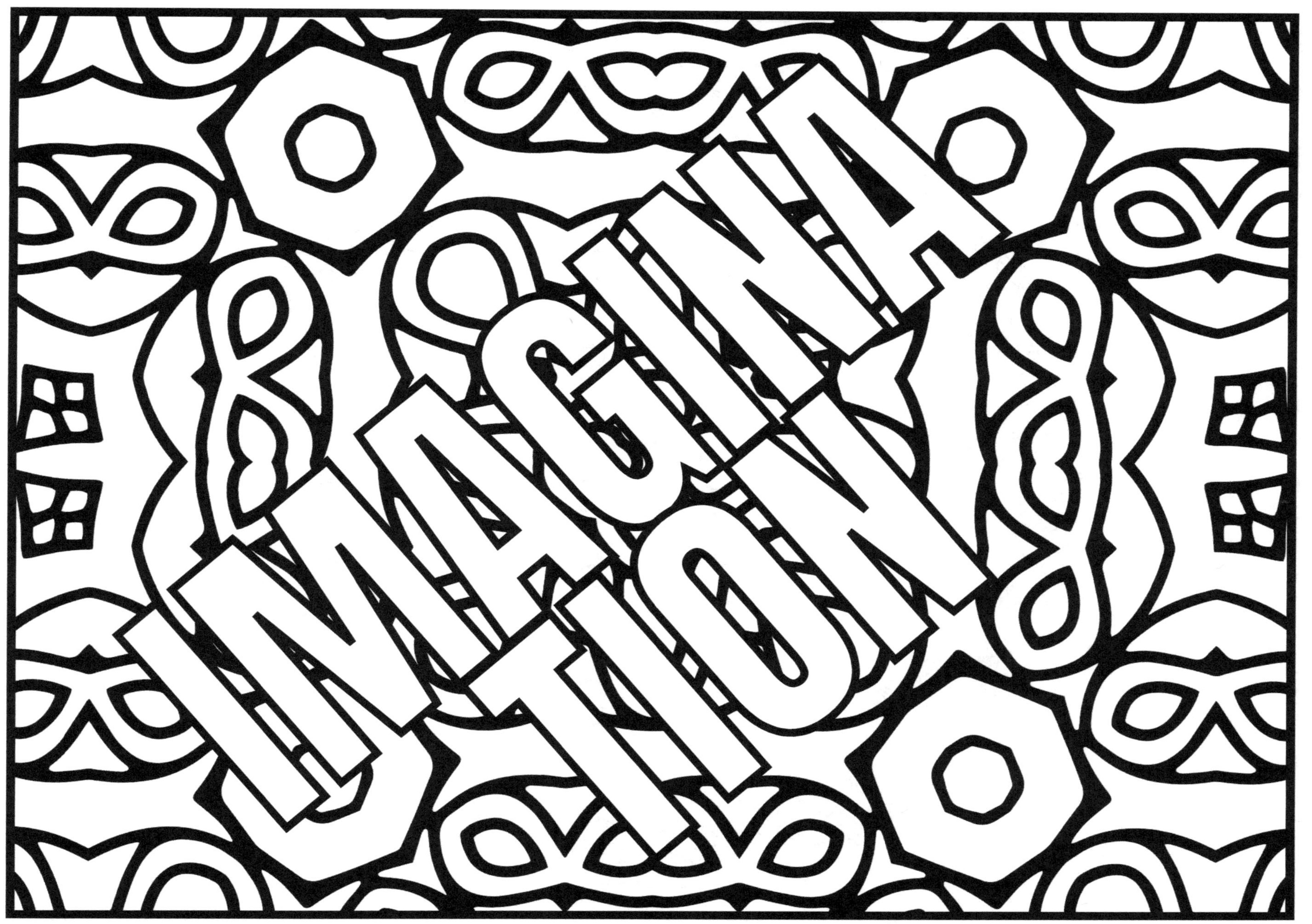
IMAGINA
TION

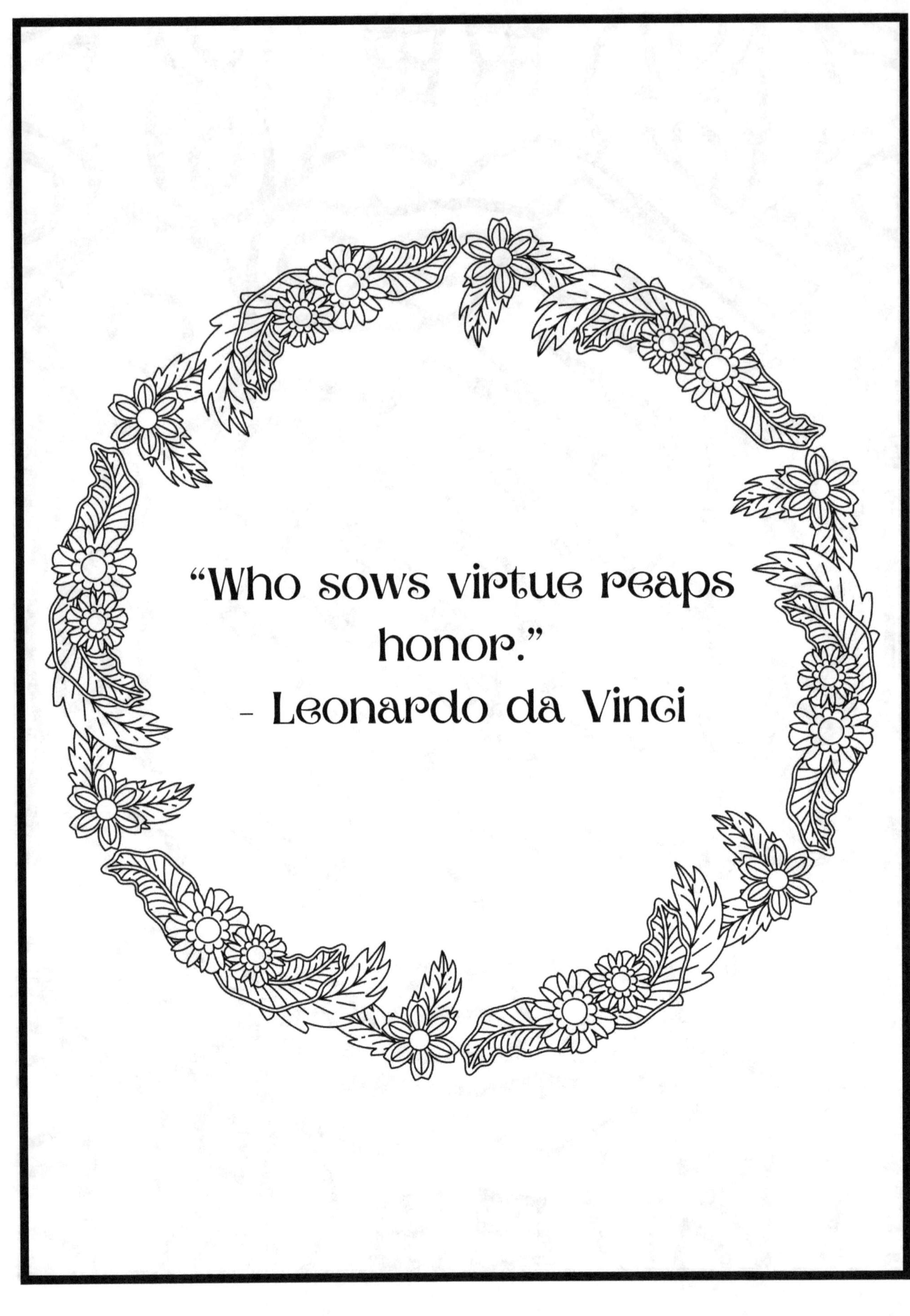
"Who sows virtue reaps honor."
- Leonardo da Vinci

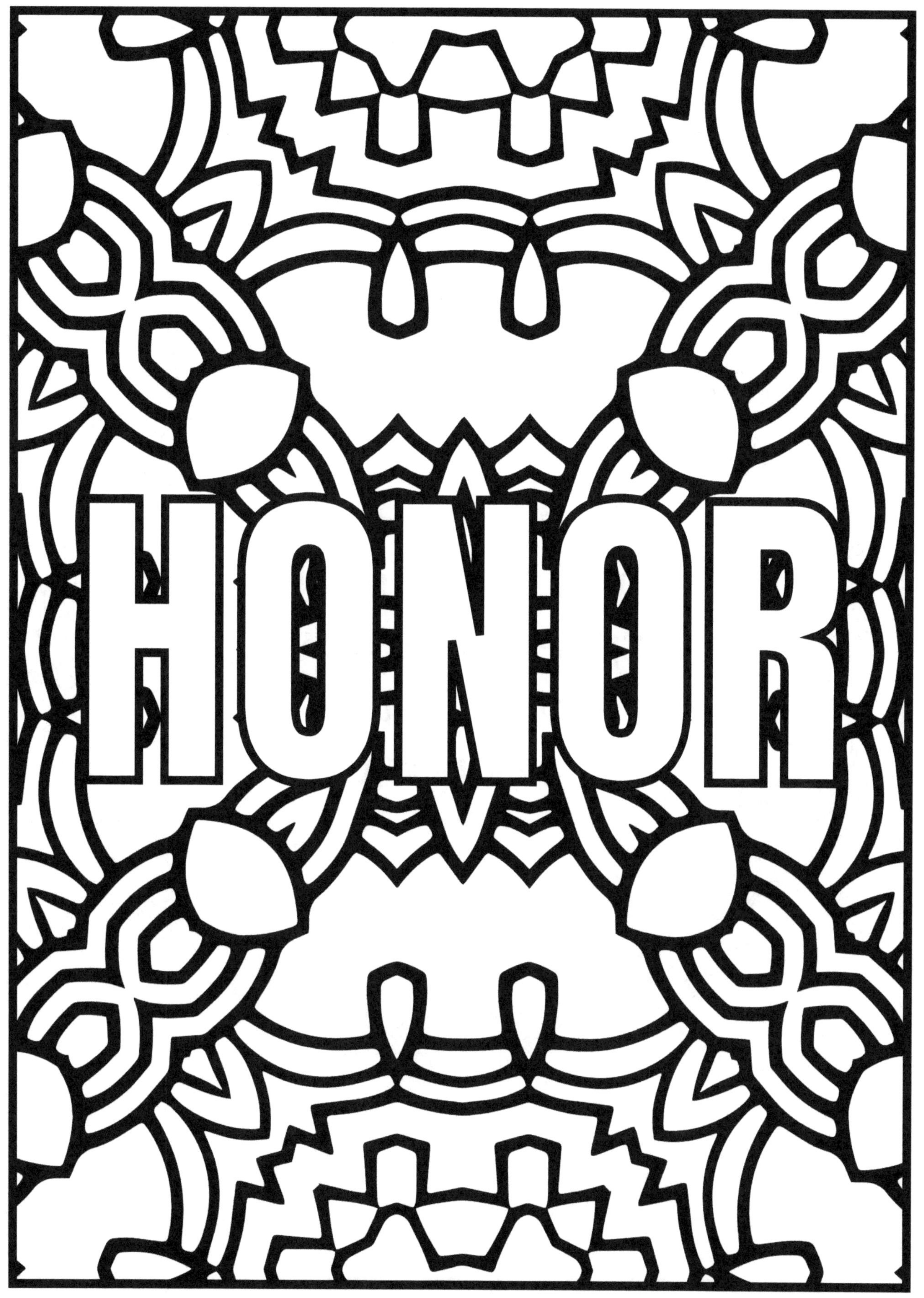
HONOR

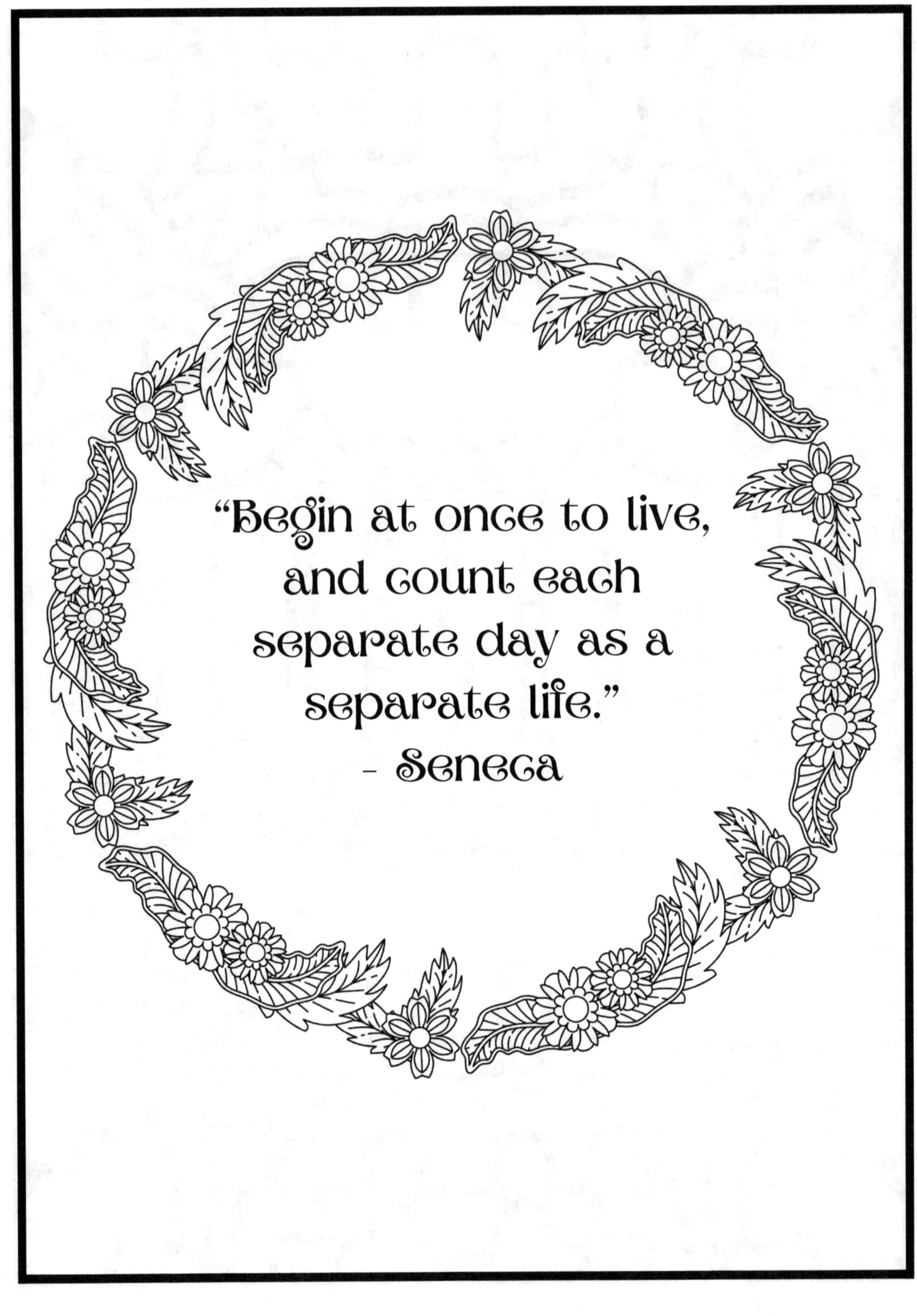
"Begin at once to live,
and count each
separate day as a
separate life."
- Seneca

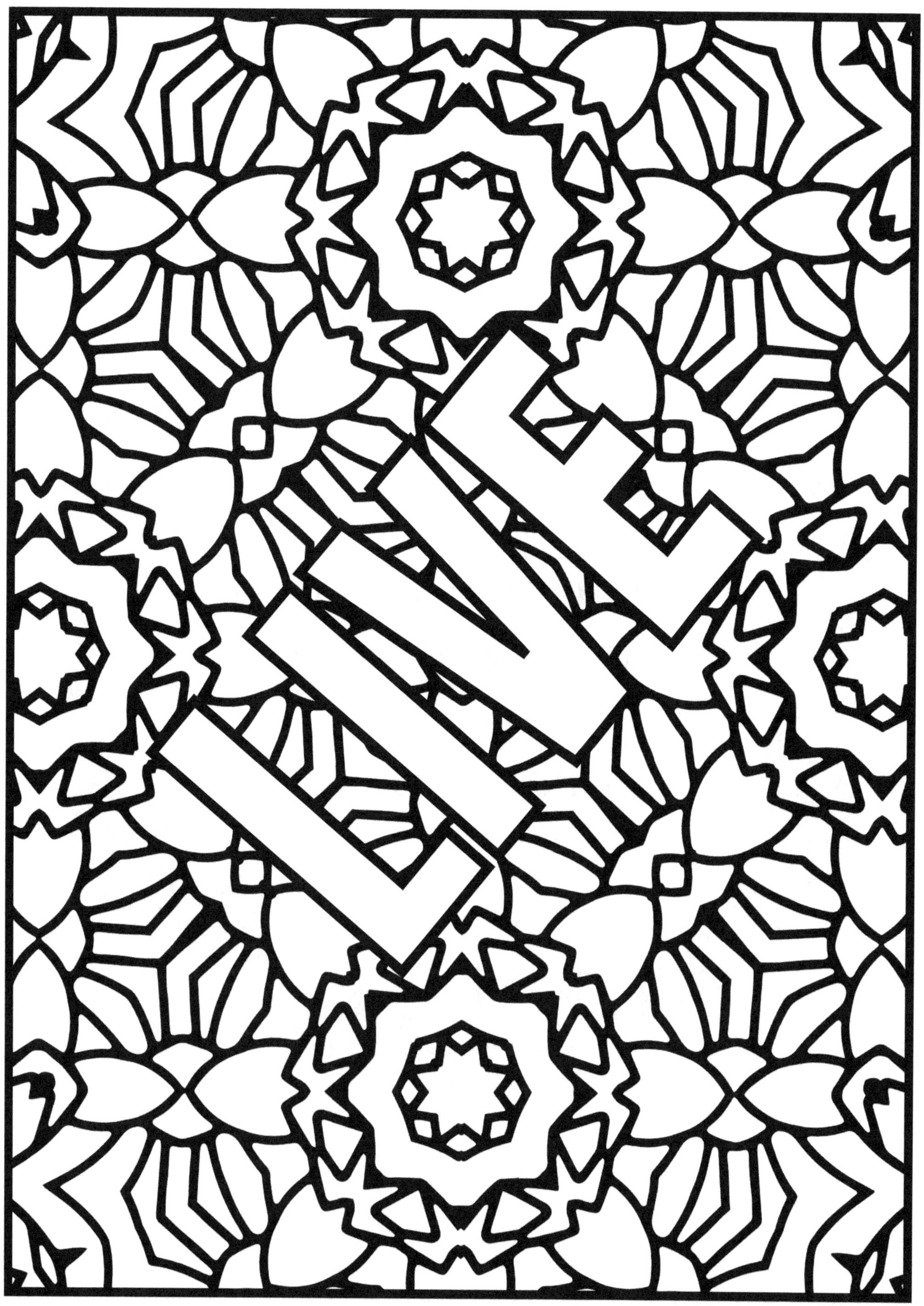
LIVE

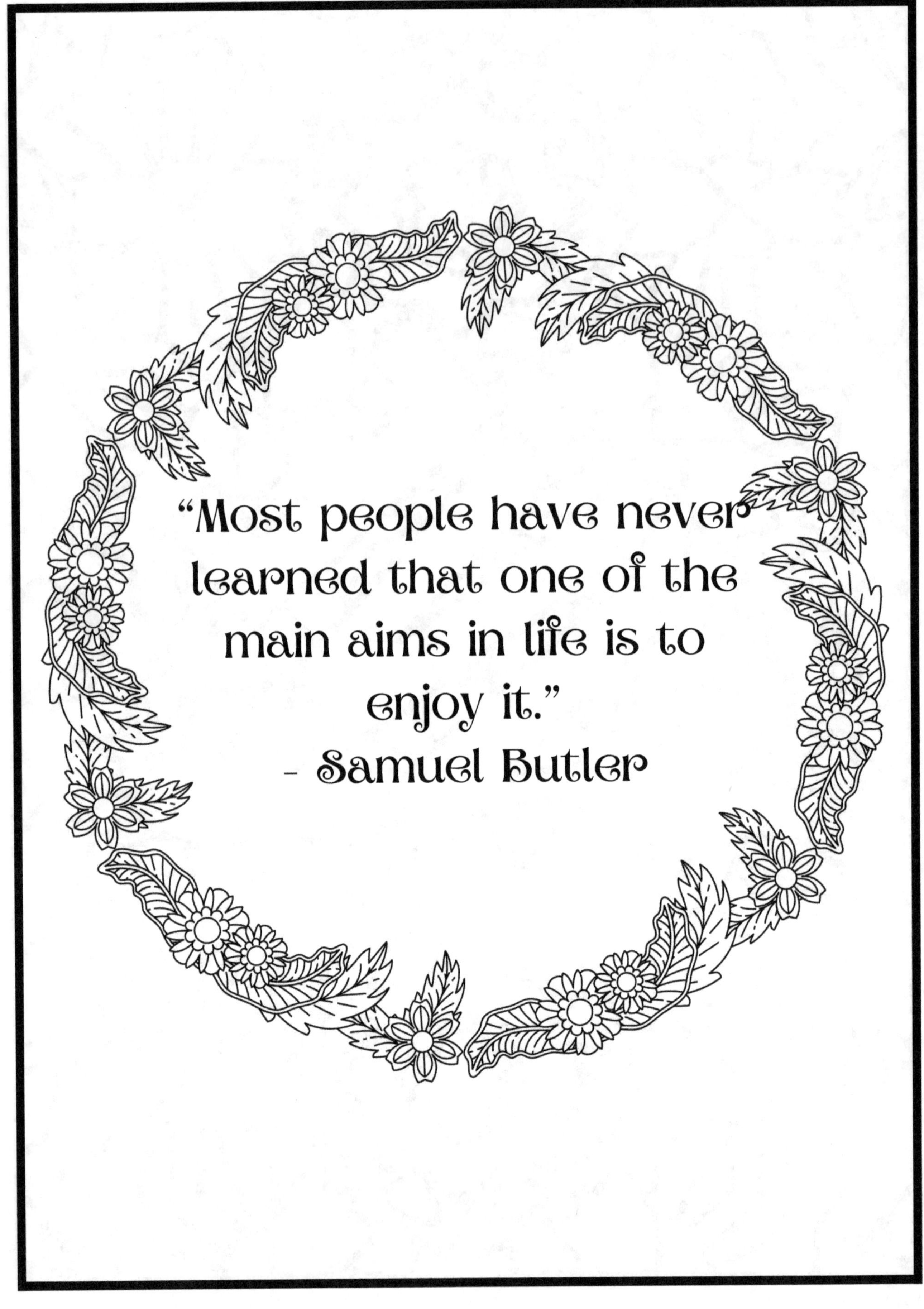
"Most people have never
learned that one of the
main aims in life is to
enjoy it."
- Samuel Butler

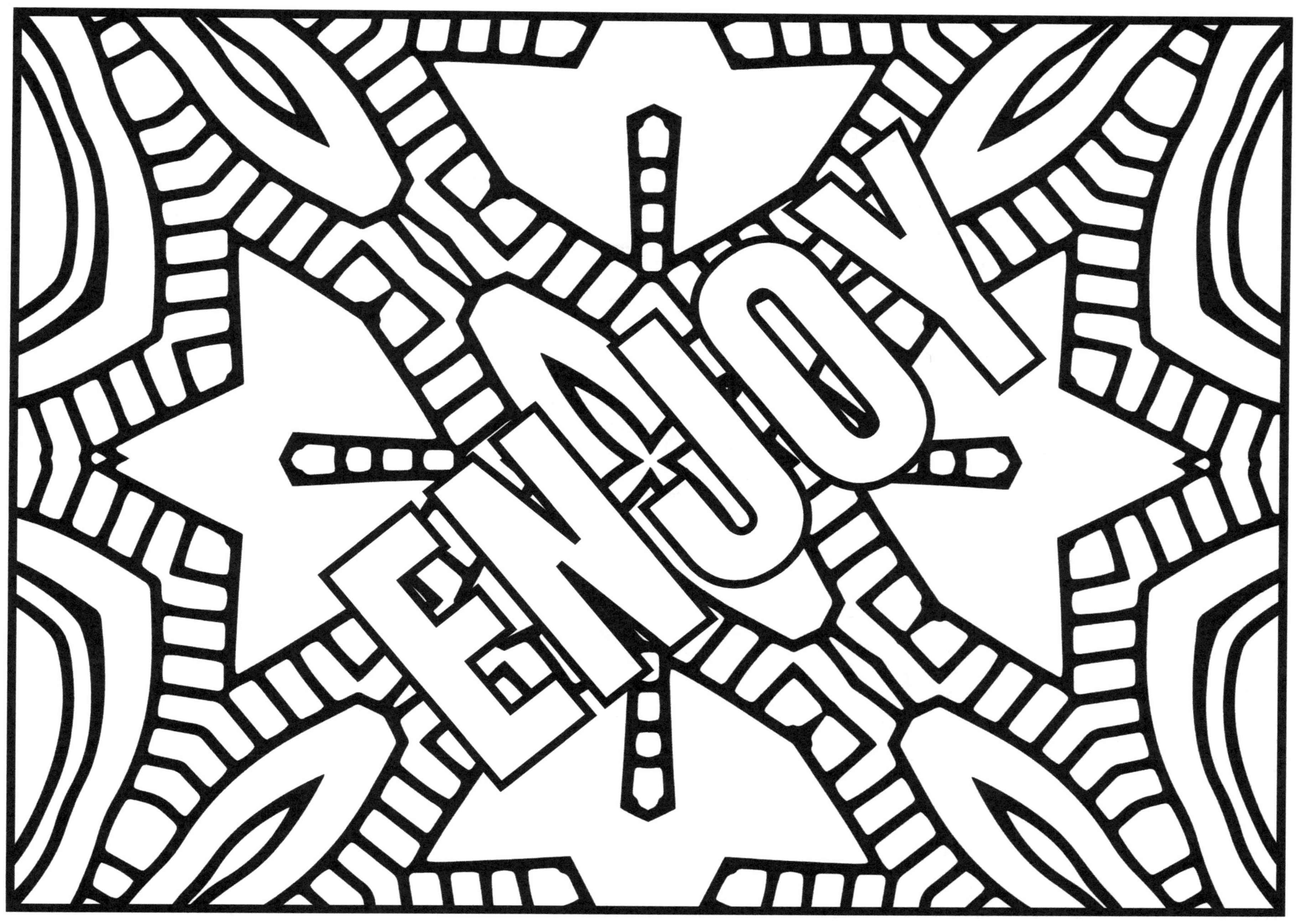
ENJOY

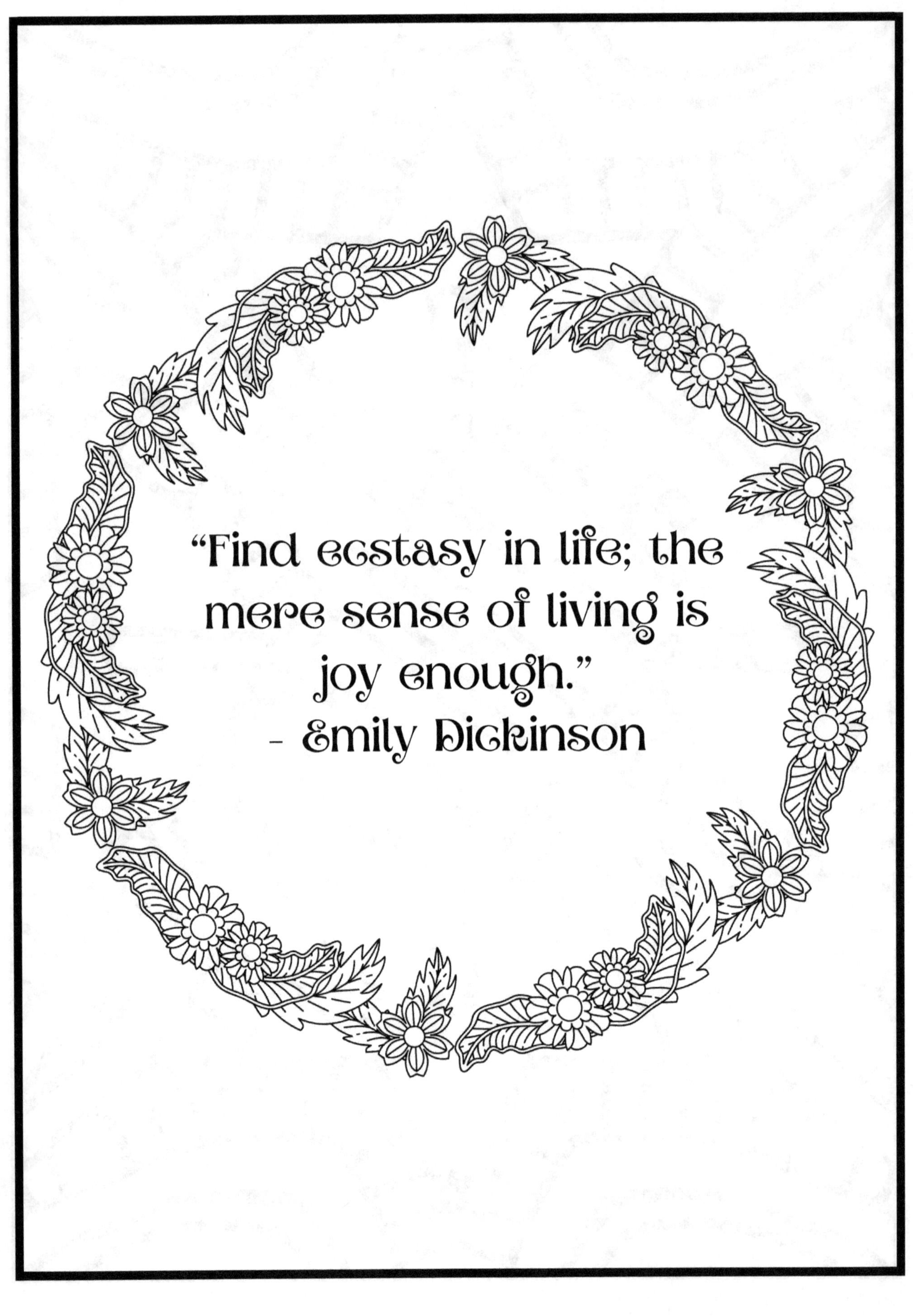
"Find ecstasy in life; the
mere sense of living is
joy enough."
- Emily Dickinson

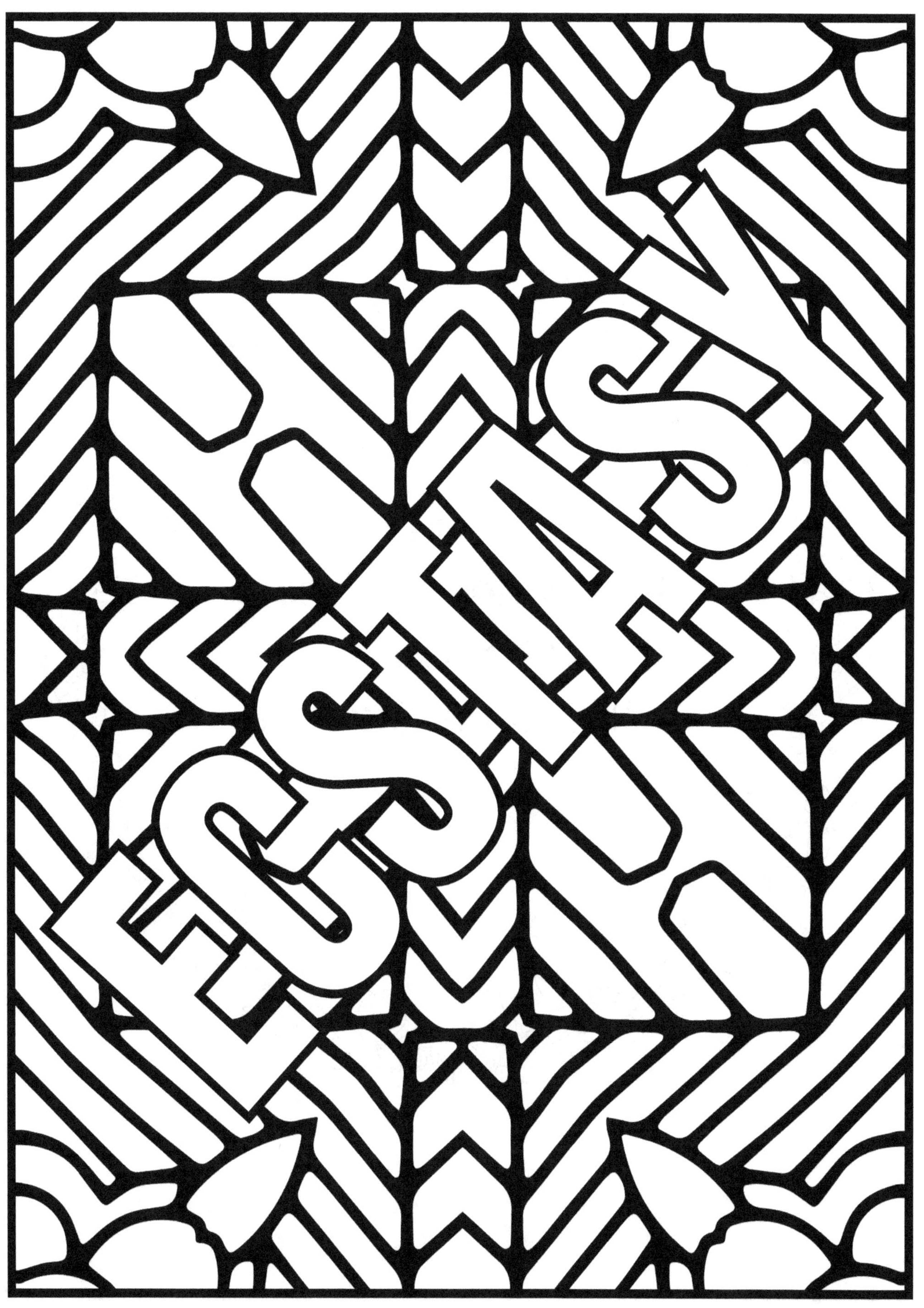
ECSTASY

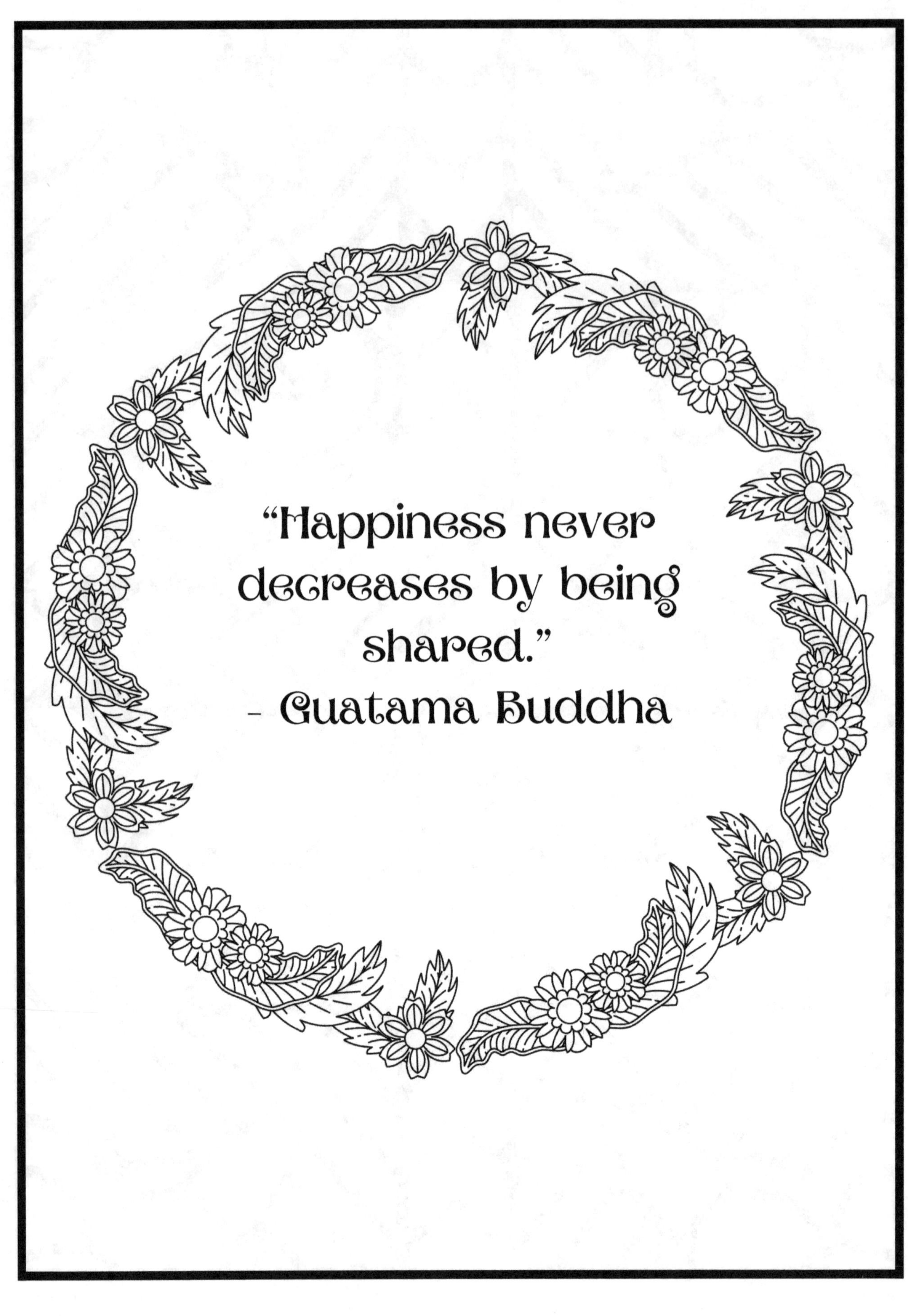
"Happiness never
decreases by being
shared."
- Guatama Buddha

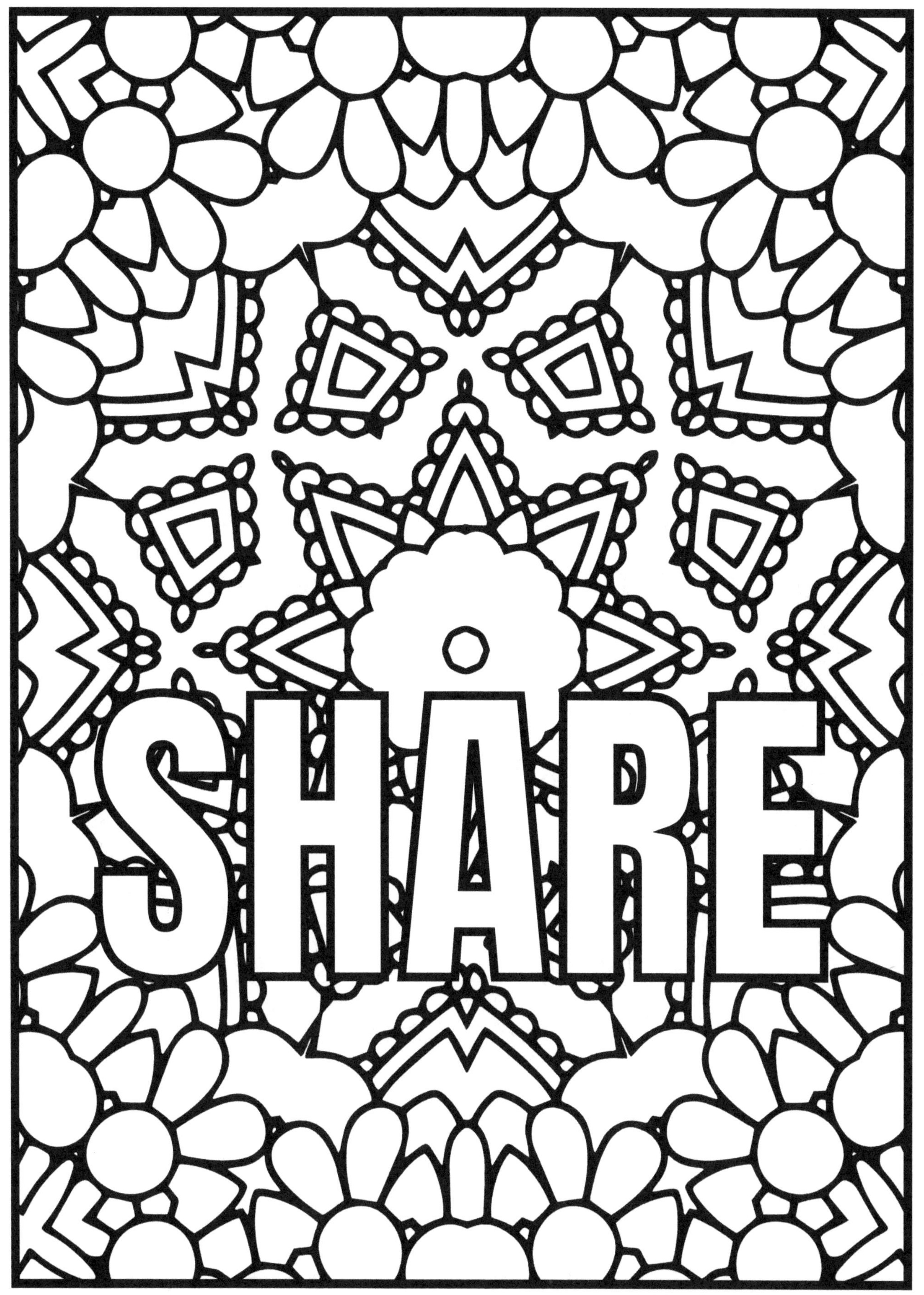
SHARE

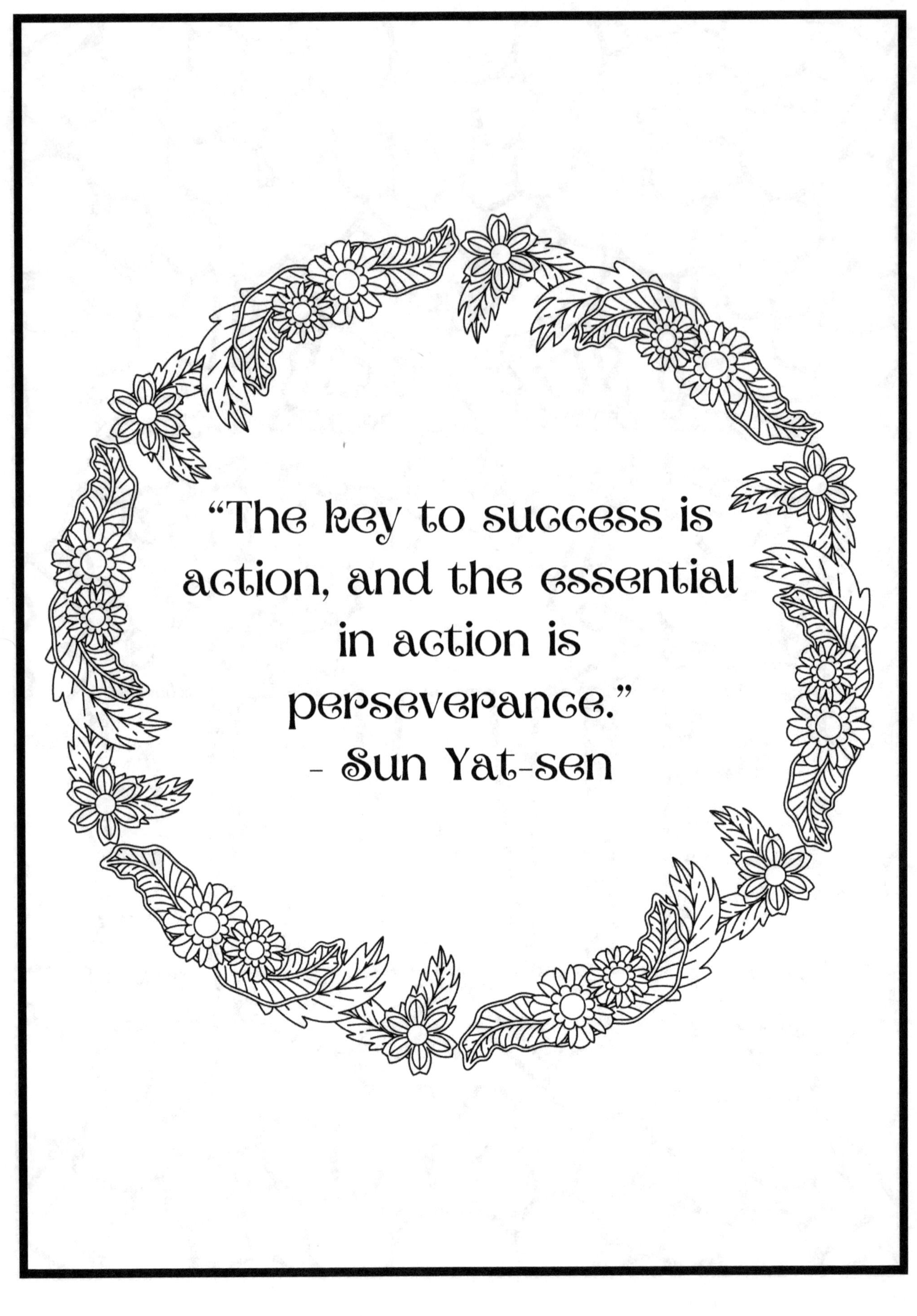
"The key to success is
action, and the essential
in action is
perseverance."
- Sun Yat-sen

www.ingramcontent.com/pod-product-compliance
Lightning Source LLC
LaVergne TN
LVHW081614110826
845155LV00039BA/193

9781951382131